Jon Smith

Start an Online Business

In easy steps is an imprint of In Easy Steps Limited
Southfield Road · Southam
Warwickshire CV47 0FB · United Kingdom
www.ineasysteps.com

Notice of Liability
Every effort has been made to ensure that this book contains accurate and current information. However, In Easy Steps Limited and the author shall not be liable for any loss or damage suffered by readers as a result of any information contained herein.

Trademarks
All trademarks are acknowledged as belonging to their respective companies.

In Easy Steps Limited supports The Forest Stewardship Council (FSC), the leading international forest certification organisation. All our titles that are printed on Greenpeace approved FSC certified paper carry the FSC logo.

MIX
Paper from
responsible sources
FSC® C020837

Printed and bound in the United Kingdom

ISBN 978-1-84078-413-8

1 Start An Online Business

So you want to run your own online business?

This chapter will explore whether you've got the determination to succeed, help you assess in which areas you may need assistance and empower you to ask the right questions.

Preparing Yourself

It's So Easy...

The media loves to over-simplify online success stories and if you've watched the news or read a newspaper over the last fifteen years you'd be forgiven for thinking that all you need for a successful e-business is a garage, an internet connection, an idea and within a matter of months you'll be selling the business for millions or floating on the stock market...

It seldom works like this. Although you will need a place to work (a garage is fine, or a kitchen table will do) an internet connection and an idea, a whole lot more goes into getting an online business off the ground and into profitability. There are numerous pitfalls to avoid and a lot of knowledge that you must gather and apply to ensure that your online business not only starts, but succeeds.

Prepare For Success

Start an Online Business In Easy Steps will show you how you can be one of the success stories rather than one of the statistics. How you can get your idea to market quickly, which features your website should include and how to market your website effectively. Whether you're intent on working full-time on your business from day one, or whether you're looking to improve your work/life balance and secure a second income, this book will walk you through the steps to creating and running a sustainable and profitable online business.

The key to a successful online business is a clear, straightforward plan, a determined entrepreneur at the helm and a dogged determination to succeed. If the answer's so simple, why is there any need to read on? Well, paradoxically building a successful online business that is both clear and straightforward is difficult and fraught with problems. Not in terms of coding or development issues; but because we like to believe that everyone thinks like we do. They don't.

Your online business needs to appeal to customers and clients possibly from a whole variety of countries, age groups and social demographics. If you're venturing into retail, then you will also need to appeal to your potential suppliers and manufacturers.

Beware

Planning a business is hard work – be prepared for late nights and frustration.

Whatever your online business, you need to stand above the competition and give your website users a very good reason to become consumers. It doesn't stop there; once they've bought from you or used your services once, you need to get them back again and again and for them to tell their friends all about you...

Don't forget

Life is all about learning. The resources listed in Chapter 8 are there to help you.

Using This Book

So how do you use this book? Well, you won't go far wrong reading it from cover to cover. Alternatively you can dip in and dip out depending on which stage you are at with your online business, it really doesn't matter. The structured approach contained within is there to guide you through to online business success. Even if your budget is modest, implementing just a handful of concepts from this book will improve your online business and will help you realize your ambitions.

Good luck on your new, exciting adventure!

Is It Right For You?

Who can start an online business? The simple answer is anyone.

This book is intended for entrepreneurs, employees, employers, mums, dads, students, existing website owners, in fact anyone interested in starting a business online no matter what their level of experience. It is for the non-techie who wants to be involved with every facet of setting up and running their own e-business – this book will show you how to research, prepare and run your own online business and will also give you the tools and the confidence to be able to explain to other staff members, clients, potential suppliers and of course customers, about what your online business is, and what it can do for them.

Hot tip

No matter what your background, with the right tools, you can succeed.

Beware

Starting an online business is not *easier* than an offline business – it's just different.

Starting an online business is by no means easier than starting a regular offline business – it still has to be well planned, it will require some funding to get you off the ground and it definitely requires hard work and determination. However, the beauty of launching online is the immediacy of your proposition being brought to market, your potential reach and access to an audience of millions all around the world. A fully functioning, all singing all dancing fully-transactional website will cost money, but nothing compared to trying to set up one or more retail units or establishing a fully-functioning comfortable office in a city-center location.

Online versus Offline:

- Relatively inexpensive to create and maintain an online presence

- Opportunity to attract a worldwide or geographically targeted audience

- Easy to give the appearance of being well-established, even if you're a new business

- Possible to compete with larger players through a clever online marketing strategy

Although there are a raft of formal qualifications available in business administration and these courses are without doubt valuable, they are not a pre-requisite to business success. Successful business owners share two things in common, the desire to succeed and the determination to turn their dream into reality.

Regardless of your socioeconomic background, your work experience, your education or your current knowledge of the online marketplace, if you have the desire and determination, you can run your own successful online business.

Don't forget

With a great design and fantastic content, it's easy to look well established.

A Little Help From A Friend...

Starting A Business With A Friend, Colleague Or Partner

Many hands make light work, so the phrase goes and it's true, having another person on board will reduce your individual workload and provide both of you with additional input, ideas, inspiration and energy.

The Positives:

- Having worked with a colleague or former colleague before, you know each other's strengths, weaknesses, skills and work ethic

- Running a business can impact the time you have to spend with your partner and family – if you're both involved you're able to enjoy time together, even though it's work

- With friends, colleagues or your partner, you have trust in each other – vitally important for the challenges you will face when running your business

- Complementing your own skills with those of a friend, colleague or partner can complete the skill sets you require to launch and run a business without having to hire externally

Beware

Just because you get on well as friends, doesn't mean you will get on well as colleagues.

12

Don't mix business with pleasure, so the phrase goes, and it's important to stress that although you might have a great personal relationship, this doesn't always transfer seamlessly into the business environment – even with colleagues who you may have spent many hours with; when it's your own venture, it's a different animal.

The Negatives:

- Problems with the business can affect your relationship with these people

- If the business fails, so too could the relationship

- Business problems will affect your personal relationship and vice versa – it's impossible to completely separate the two

- Personal commitments or enthusiasm for the business can change with time, those changes may not always be compatible.

Don't forget

You can always invite a partner into the business once it's established.

If you do decide to run a business with a friend, family member partner or former colleague, formalize the business relationship from the start – list the responsibilities, investment requirements, the split of ownership, remuneration levels and what happens if the business and/or the relationship should fail. It's not a pleasant experience, but just blind faith that everything will be fine, is dangerous for the business and for you as individuals.

Some of the most successful and highly visible online success stories happened through partnerships between friends, colleagues or couples. You can do it too – but tread carefully.

Why Start A Business?

Why On Earth Would You Want To Start An Online Business?

Well, other than the potential financial returns, running an online business is hugely rewarding, and, once established it can offer you a plethora of additional benefits in addition to income. Many online businesses begin in the owner's home, significantly reducing travel time and cost. The time saved from not commuting plus a freedom to work the hours you choose, will also drastically improve your work/life balance. Working for yourself by definition puts you in charge of your own destiny. Creating something from scratch is tough, but launching your own venture is emotionally rewarding and instills a tremendous feeling of accomplishment. The path you are about to embark on will be a challenge, but if you've got the required determination, anything is possible.

Hot tip

Choose one evening a week for non-work activities – and stick to it!

Beware

The work/life balance comes with time. Initially it's going to be more work than rest!

A Reality Check

If all you need is desire and determination, surely anyone can run a business? Not really, running your own online business is hard work. There's no way to gloss over this fact, and it would be naïve to believe that all that stands in your way of online business success is a matter of time.

Preparing, launching and running your online business will stretch your resolve. When things are going well, it's easy to be positive and to be optimistic about the future. But life and business isn't that straightforward, you're going to take knocks even during the business planning stage and it takes a certain character to be able to react to these situations and still find the determination to proceed.

Your relationships with friends and family will change, not least because of the time you will need to dedicate to the business. If you're running the business in addition to paid employment then all that leisure time you enjoyed in the evenings or weekends will now be spent hunched over a laptop or spreadsheets. If you're working on the business full time, then it really does mean full time – emails and calls will remain unanswered unless you're there to communicate. Running your own business is not 9-5, five days a week. Support from friends and family is essential to your business success and their understanding of your commitment and goals are essential.

Running a business means working to a budget, both professionally and personally. It's unlikely in the first few years of operations that you will be able to afford (the cost or the time) holidays, meals out, an extensive new wardrobe or your usual monthly treats. Your new business will take over your life!

Still think that running your own online business is for you? Great, well let's get started.

Don't forget

Friends will be happy to support you – if you remember to ask!

15

Carving Out A Niche

With the best will in the world, saying "I want to be the next Amazon" is not going to work. Amazon enjoys a huge market share, incredible buying power and offers a vast range of products and services across a number of verticals. It wasn't always that way. Amazon had to start somewhere and it started by selling books and only books. The behemoth you see now is the expansion of an online book retailer that became expert in analyzing a market, building supplier relations, investing in technology, processes and customer services and of course marketing. Only when the model was proven through books, was the company able to expand into new products and services.

Hot tip

Your niche doesn't have to be original, it just has to be targeted.

Beware

One USP isn't enough – you need to appeal to customers on multiple levels.

Amazon filled a niche – and that niche was to offer customers the largest possible range of book titles (over 1 million at the time) which dwarfed even the largest physical bookstore offering some 100,000 titles.

What will ensure the success of your online business is your clear understanding and obsessive approach to the product or service niche you intend to dominate.

Less is more, and deciding upon a niche, empowers your entire business – the marketing, the positioning, the branding and the messaging to customers. Specializing in a specific product or service range, allows you to dominate – spread yourself too thin and your business will be a jack of all, master of none…

Defining Your USPs

No business is truly unique the same way that no movie plot is truly original. What makes a successful movie is the unique combination of great script, cast, crew, market conditions and the right budget and marketing. It's the same for successful businesses. As a business owner, you will be providing services or products online. The same products or services are already available on the market. Your job is to sell or provide those products in a different way to all of the other competitors on the market. You will still need to get the basics right – great website, great sales and marketing, customer services and of course provide a quality product or service… but how you define your business as being different to all the others, and how you market those differences in the form of Unique Selling Points, is what will give your business the unique combination it needs for success.

Don't forget

Check out what the competition is offering – is there something you can do better?

- Faster or cheaper (or free!) shipping

- The most comprehensive product or service offering

- Specialist, industry recognized or expert knowledge in your field

- Fully qualified staff

- *x*-number of years' offline experience

- Generous/interest-free or innovative payment terms for clients

- Hand made or limited edition products

- Cheapest or most exclusive pricing

- Money-back guarantee

- Price match promise

- Invite-only membership/registration

Even if there are thousands of competitors selling the same or similar, even if they have been operating for a lot longer than you and even if they command larger marketing budgets, your business will gain customers if you can clearly identify the USPs that differentiate your business from the competition and help you carve your niche. Your USPs may not be immediately obvious to you, don't worry, this is all part of the business planning process.

Good Times, Bad Times

Is The Time Right?

The economy is both part of, and the cause of, a constant cycle which means there will always be 'good times' and 'bad times'. Current economic circumstances are trying indeed. Banks are being very cautious with their depleted cash reserves and for those of you looking for business loans there is simply less to go around. Risk averse lenders demand more security and will scrutinize business plans in more detail. This is not necessarily a bad thing – the additional pressure to work on your numbers until they are right can only help ensure you've planned your business well, have researched your market sufficiently and the bank agrees with you that your business has a reasonable chance of success.

Beware

If you negotiate too hard, you run the risk of alienating potential suppliers – be firm but fair.

There is an argument that businesses started during an economic downturn are in a far stronger position to weather any future slumps and because they're built leaner and smarter, can capitalize on growth opportunities when things are on the up.

A depressed economy also means that any services or products you require to set up and run your business can be found more competitively priced; vendors will often enhance their service to win and retain your business and as cruel as it may sound, you can benefit from other failing businesses by buying up their liquidated stock, hiring their staff or picking up reasonably priced office and technical equipment to get your own business off the ground.

Is the time right? If you are planning to sell a product or service that customers need or want, yes it is.

Knowing Your Skills...

Don't forget

Paying for outside assistance isn't a weakness – it's good business strategy.

We can all multi task and through experience, education and human nature we possess lots of skills that will help us to run an online business. But no one is an expert in all aspects and whatever your expertise, you will require additional assistance with the planning, development and deployment of your online business.

Knowing and understanding your skills, and more importantly recognizing the gaps in your knowledge is a sometimes painful self-assessment, but one which done correctly will reap rewards throughout your entrepreneurial experience.

Although it's critical for your cash flow, especially during the start up phase, to manage your costs; accepting your limitations and paying for expert help when necessary will not only get your project moving forward quickly, but will ensure that your project stands the best chance of success now and in the future. Just like with building a house, a solid business is built on solid foundations.

Being a successful business owner does not always mean doing everything yourself – in fact, being a successful business owner means knowing how and when to make the decision to 'do it yourself' or to 'manage internal/external resources'.

Understanding Business

Let's look at the major functions of a business. Of course depending on the product or service you wish to provide online your focus and requirements will differ, but every business will require skills and elements of the following disciplines:

Sales, Marketing & PR

Often lumped together, Sales, Marketing and PR are complex disciplines which must be deployed successfully for your business to succeed. As a service provider, finding prospects, communicating your offering and closing the sale are your business's chief concern. You may well be an accomplished accountant or insurance broker, but if you're shy, better with numbers than words or lack the necessary 'people skills' to close a deal, your business will not grow.

Beware

Marketing your website is a huge task – you're probably going to need help.

If you're providing products or services to businesses or consumers, you're going to need to let your target audience know you exist through both on- and offline marketing strategies. Customers want information, prices, images of the products, guarantees that the product will arrive and it will work… If you're busy shipping products or dealing with customer service issues, who's managing your Google Adwords campaign, or copy writing a press release?

Analyze your strengths and weaknesses in Sales, Marketing and PR. Will you require additional assistance now or in the future? If so, research some of the services on offer from other companies and research the salaries being paid to staff in these disciplines and what sort of skills they could bring to your business. Keep notes, you're building up vital data to help with your business plan and financial projections.

Front-end Development, Back-End Development, Hosting, Systems Administration, Database Development And Administration...

By nature of the fact that your business is online, there will be a technical component to your business; at the very least a website and an email account. How deep you want to be involved with the technical function will depend mainly on your background and interest. It is of course completely possible to operate an online business with absolutely no knowledge of the internet market or the technologies required. If you're not sure what exactly some of the skills listed above actually are, chances are you'll be employing a third party to develop and maintain your website. This is very sensible and far more effective than trying to teach yourself HTML and the complexities of server configuration and maintenance. Outsourcing your technical functions will cost money, but if you get the 'online' bit of your online business wrong, well, the future's not very bright...

In your search for a technical partner, it's imperative that you make it clear how much or how little technical involvement you require in building, deploying and maintaining your website.

Don't forget

It's totally possible to run a successful online business even if you're not 'technical'.

21

...cont'd

Legal

The legal peculiarities of the internet deserve a book in their own right. Although the internet embodies and empowers everything we understand about globalization and free trade, sadly someone forgot to tell the lawmakers...

Operating an online business has legal implications for both you and your business. Depending on where the company is registered, where and what you sell, to whom you sell (consumers or business) make every online business at least partially unique. It's strongly recommended you seek professional legal help when creating your online business to make sure you and your company stay on the right side of the law. No matter what your product or service, as a bare minimum, you will need to display website terms and conditions and your privacy policy. If you're selling products overseas, you'll need to be aware of countries you are forbidden to trade to because of government embargoes and depending on the products you are selling, which territories you are licensed to trade within, especially in relation to consumer electronics and entertainment/media products.

Finance

The heart and soul of each and every company, the effective management and reporting of financial matters make the difference between a good idea and a great business. It is fairly common to be successful without being an economist, but without doubt knowing your numbers makes for more accurate forecasts, effective cash flow and long term success.

As a limited company you are obliged to submit annual accounts and it is strongly recommended you employ an accountant to manage this process if you have little or no experience in this field.

Engaging an accountant from the point of just planning your business affords you access to advice, recommendations and financial strategy which can radically improve your business plan, assist with raising finance and ensure your personal income tax and company sales tax/VAT liabilities are correctly measured and accounted for.

Hot tip

Look for legal document templates on the web, but customize for your own specific needs.

Beware

Don't cut and paste terms and privacy policy from another site – create your own.

Operations, Supply Chain, Distribution

If you're planning to sell physical products through your online business, this is an enormously important aspect of your business. The sourcing, storing, pricing and distribution of products becomes ever more complex the larger your range and the larger your customer base.

Don't overlook how long it takes to receive, bin, pick, pack and ship individual products. Your storage facility needs to be fit for purpose and if you're planning to operate the business alone, what happens if there's a delivery and you're out at meetings all day, or you receive customer orders but you're on holiday all week?

Hiring staff or employing a warehousing and distribution firm needs to be considered.

Don't forget

If you're planning to store stock in your home, ensure the area is dry, clean and secure.

Customer Services/Account Management/Customer Relationship Management

Often overlooked by start-up organizations, your commitment to customers speaks volumes about how customers will perceive and engage with your business and invariably will influence your long-term success. Communicating with customers, liaising about existing projects or orders, and maintaining customer relationships now and in the future takes a significant amount of time and effort. If you're dealing with customer service issues, you're not chasing new prospects, and vice versa. Start thinking about your strategy and how you will manage this aspect of your business. Again, you can hire staff or utilise 3rd party customer service solutions. This needs to be budgeted for and the research and costs reflected in your business planning.

External Help And Advice

Hot tip

If you contribute to forums a lot, you tend to receive better responses to your own questions.

Beware

Whenever you're seeking advice, only release the minimum amount of information required.

The UK government, budget cuts allowing, provide the Business Link service to UK-based businesses. Registering at www.businesslink.gov.uk will give you access to a large, constantly updated database of information that covers all aspects of planning and operating a business in the UK. Business Link have regional offices which provide phone support and consultancy services all completely free of charge. In addition, they organise events covering specific topics such as Sales Strategies or Online Marketing which are valuable both in terms of content and for networking opportunities. Take a look also at the Federation of Small Businesses (www.fsb.org.uk) and the British Chamber of Commerce (www.britishchambers.org.uk).

Social Network Help

Social Networking websites such as Linked In and Xing are incredibly useful both in terms of sourcing potential suppliers, partners and customers and because of the Groups function which offers the chance to become part of a group of like-minded industry players. There are groups for start up entrepreneurs, groups that cater for specific industries or products and groups that focus on online marketing and e-commerce etc.

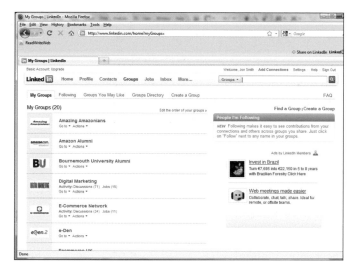

Don't forget

Make sure your Linked In or Xing profile is complete and up to date.

Don't be afraid to ask for help or advice. There is no shame in approaching others – they were all in exactly the same position as you. The worst thing somebody can say is, no.

The world is full of useful and helpful people and if you search hard enough, it's quite possible to find answers to your questions and concerns, completely free of charge.

An informed entrepreneur is a successful entrepreneur and without a shadow of a doubt, the hours you put into finding out information now will make the process of planning, launching and operating your online business all the more fluid.

Chapter Summary

- Starting an online business is tough, but with determination, and a complete understanding of what you want to do online, it's possible

- Prepare yourself and your family/friends for the time commitment starting a new online business requires

- However, remember to allow yourself some free time, so you don't alienate your nearest and dearest

- Seek and accept assistance from whomever and wherever you can, be it free, paid for or bartered

- The online marketplace is busy – differentiate yourself from the competition with clear USPs and carve out a niche for yourself

- Starting an online business requires a lot of skills, some of which you won't have. Pay professionals to keep your project on track

- Working with a partner can reduce the workload, but proceed with caution

- New businesses can prosper during hard times if you negotiate hard for any products, services or skills you require

- Remain customer-focused at all times, or you won't run a business for very long

- Know and understand your numbers – the heart and soul of every business are the financials

- If you're planning to sell products online, budget accordingly for the resources required (time, money and staff) of receiving, storing and distributing stock

2 Business Planning & Finance

A successful business needs to be well planned and adequately financed – this chapter will explore how to plan, why you should plan and what needs to be done to get your business up and running as well as your options for raising seed capital from a variety of different sources.

Business Planning

What's All The Fuss?

You can look at writing a business plan in two ways. To appease a lender, so that you can raise the necessary finance, or, to create a working document that helps you plan, launch and execute a well thought out and well run enterprise.

A business plan is of course essential if you are looking to raise finance, whether it's from a bank, a business angel or a friend or family member. Whoever you approach is going to want to see what your business will do, who's involved, how it's going to attract customers, how much money you're planning to make and how much money you are planning to spend now and in the future. But fundamentally you should write a business plan for yourself.

There are some great online resources and tools available to help you create a business plan, along with a huge selection of books on the subject. There is no right or wrong way to write and present a business plan, but without doubt the best business plans cover the essential information identified below, and no matter what you call the section, or which font or point size you decide upon, a well written business plan should convey to an outsider:

- **The What?** The business aims, goals and objectives

- **The Who?** The management and staff behind the venture, the size and nature of the customer base

- **The Why?** The market need for the business and how this business will sit in the market

- **The How?** The strategy for launch and beyond, the money, the systems and the processes

Hot tip

MS Word includes a Business Plan template document you can use to get started.

Beware

Concentrate on function over form – make sure the content is strong, not just the design.

The What? Business Aims, Goals And Objectives

It may seem obvious, but start your business plan with a statement of intent – what is it your business will do, what services or products are being provided? What is the business called, where do you plan to take the business in one, two and three years?

The Who? Identifying And Understanding Your Market

Deciding what you want to sell or provide online is of course key to getting your online business operational, but before you spend one single penny on your website or on products, you must identify your market. The internet is of course a great place to start. The abundance of data, including the search terms people use, the age and demographics of buyers/users of your services or products and the opportunity to connect with potential partners, suppliers, customers and clients means that no stone need be left unturned.

- Customer Profiling – identify the age, gender, socioeconomic background and potential frequency of purchases you can expect from your client base. This information is critical when you plan your business and forecast your pricing and revenue.

- Product or service life cycle – does what you are planning to sell or provide allow the opportunity to re-sell to the same customer again in the future? Can you offer upgrades or enhancements? Is there an opportunity to sell multiple products or services at the same time, to the same customer? How often will they need to replace this product or service? Is there a limited lifespan on the product or service, how many do you plan to sell and how many will you hold in stock?

- Price point/elasticity – what pricing will the market tolerate? Are you aiming for few high-value sales, or multiple low-value sales? What does the competition do and how do you want to be perceived by the market?

- Client life cycle – is your product or service tailored or suited to a particular age range? Does your product or service adapt itself it to different age ranges?

The Why? And The How?

The Why? Market Needs And How Your Business Will Satisfy Them

Your business will only succeed if you are satisfying a market need. People must want or need the product or service you provide; without demand, it's going to be much more of an uphill struggle. Don't lose heart if you're planning to introduce something new or untried into the marketplace – look at Facebook… who would have predicted that over half a billion people (at last count) would require regular access to a website that in its simplest form, allows users to post snippets of information about their lives?

The Market

Understanding the market is more complicated than it might first appear. Markets are fickle and change happens quickly. Above all else, you and everyone you know is a consumer – do people you know want or need the product or service you are planning to provide? Do others? How many and how often? Ask yourself these questions, and use the internet and other sources to work out the size of your market and its value.

Your Proposition

In chapter 1 we looked at defining your USPs and carving a niche for your business. As these begin to take shape in your mind, it's time to use them to effect in your business planning. How do you market these USPs? How will you convey your USPs to potential customers? Is the niche you've chosen competitive or relatively untapped? How will you let users know of your business's existence?

Hot tip

Professional research can cost money – it's a worthwhile expense for the insights provided.

Beware

Your USPs can easily be copied by competitors; ensure there's more to your business than 'cheap' prices.

The How? A Strategy For Launch And Beyond

Having the business idea, in a sense, is the easy bit. Actually delivering on your business plan is a whole different thing. Turning your business dream into a reality is a long, complicated process that requires some serious work on your behalf. Don't lose heart, if you plan correctly and within that plan outline exactly how it is you intend to launch and run the business, you will make your life much easier.

The Money

Business is all about making money – not every business will make millions, nor does it need to, to be deemed a success. Maybe your goal is to achieve a better work/life balance or just work in an industry that you know or love. Whatever your ambitions, clear financial goals and objectives, coupled with accurate forecasting, financial record-keeping and keeping a keen eye on your cash flow will all help you achieve business success.

Don't forget

Search the web for Open Source software to assist you.

31

The Systems

Systems and processes need to be in place for a reason – to help you get stuff done. Plan right from the start how you will market to customers, retain customers and communicate with customers. The same with suppliers and service providers. How do you plan to record your stock levels, transactions and customer service issues? How exactly will customers navigate on your website and what actually happens when a customer orders a product or service from you? Of course your processes and systems will alter and improve over time, but you need a baseline to begin with.

Competitive Analysis

Who sells what you sell? How much do they sell it for? Where do you want to position yourself – as the cheapest or one of them, somewhere in the middle, top end or the most exclusive?

Competition is a fact of life – we're in competition from the moment we're born until we die. Business is no different. Someone, somewhere, sells or provides the products or services that you plan to.

What are their USPs, can you offer similar or better?

What about qualifications, years of experience, staff numbers?

When analyzing your competitors, always play the part of a consumer, look at their messaging and the site layout. Study how the products or services are presented and the use of language to communicate with customers.

If it's appropriate, order a product or a service and pay particular attention to the process, how long the delivery takes, the choice of courier, the package and it's contents, the invoice/receipt, whether the package contains promotional material for themselves or a 3rd party advertiser.

Ask your competitor questions via email or their online form, what are their response times and the quality of the information received? Can you offer the same or better?

Take honest and accurate results. Grade your competitors using a score sheet and pay particular attention to the areas in which they let themselves down, and the areas in which they excel. This analysis provides you with an accurate baseline. If you are going to win market share, you will need to offer the same or better on every count. Customers are inadvertently conducting competitive analysis every time they engage with a website, and they flock to the businesses that offer the best service.

Exit Strategy

An exit strategy is an indication of how you plan to leave the company in the medium to long term. It may seem counter-productive to include a statement regarding your own future involvement with the company, but actually lenders appreciate that you've thought of a possible future scenario, and they themselves will be assessing the exit routes open to them.

An exit strategy could be a:

- **Merger** – planning from the start to create an attractive company that could be incorporated into another company – often because your business offers complementary products or services, or your market share or customer base is of particular interest to another firm.

- **Acquisition** – planning from the start to create an attractive company that could be bought out by another company – often for the same reasons as a merger, but in these instances the acquiring company is intent on incorporating your staff, skills and/or customer base or in some cases simply suppressing your brand.

- **Trade sale** – planning from the start to create an attractive company that could be bought out by another company, group or individual – this often results in the brand continuing under new management after your exit.

- **Flotation** – planning from the start to create an attractive company that will list on the stock market, appeal to investors and offer them the opportunity to profit from the success of your business.

Even if, at the moment, you have absolutely no intention of selling the business, include an exit strategy stating that the business is intending to remain with the same ownership for the foreseeable future.

Don't forget

It's not uncommon to include competitor websites in your list of potential buyers.

Financial Documents

By law, companies are required to produce financial statements each year. These statements appear in your Company Reports and are available publicly (for a nominal fee). There are two main financial statements, namely The Profit and Loss Account and The Balance Sheet. Producing both, and more importantly understanding both documents and the accounting principles behind them will help you in the day-to-day running of your business.

The Profit And Loss (P&L) Account

This account can be updated regularly and shows how much profit or loss a business is making. With all the correct figures to hand, it is a simple calculation. Profit can be gross profit or net profit.

Gross profit = Turnover - Cost of Sales

Net Profit = Gross Profit - Expenses

A business is making a loss if the above calculation results in a negative figure.

Turnover is sometimes referred to as sales revenue and is calculated by multiplying the number of items sold (or services provided) by the price you charge customers. Cost of Sales refers to the costs directly associated with the products you sell, for example the price you pay for your stock.

Overheads are usually referred to as expenses in the P&L account and typical expenses for an online business include items such as website hosting and rent costs, as well as marketing and insurance. General administrative costs of running a business appear as administrative expenses and the cost of staff is recorded under Salaries.

Hot tip

If you haven't got MS Excel, check out an alternative from OpenOffice.org.

The Balance Sheet

The Balance Sheet is a snapshot taken at a particular moment in time, giving a summary of the overall financial position of the business.

Businesses need to utilize assets in order to generate wealth. Assets are the things that a business owns or sums of money that are owed to the business at any one moment in time.

The business obtains the finance for these assets from two main sources:

- Internally (inside the business) from capital raised from the business owners (the shareholders in the case of a company).

- Externally in the form of bank loans, and other forms of finance which will need to be repaid.

When you set up a business, the business becomes a legal body in its own right. Internal finance (shareholders' funds) is owed to shareholders.

External finance is owed to people outside the business - liabilities.

The Balance Sheet will therefore balance because, in simple terms, this shows that the value of a business's assets is financed by the two groups – 1. Internal (owner's capital), 2. External (liabilities).

A balance sheet typically appears in a vertical format.

The balance sheet starts off by listing all the assets. Next, come the liabilities. Finally, the owners' capital is shown – to balance the balance sheet.

Search [balance sheet template download] to start working on your own balance sheet.

Don't forget

No matter how informed your projections, update once you have real sales data.

Registering Your Business

Once you've decided that you want to start your own online business, you will need to make a decision about the legal structure of your business and begin the registration process; this can be done in conjunction with your business planning and must be complete before you begin to trade.

Each structure has differing legal implications for you and the business so it's essential to choose the one that is a best fit for your business and you. Below we'll explore your options:

- Sole Trader (UK)

- Limited Liability Company – Sole proprietorship (USA)

- Limited Liability Company (UK/USA)

- Partnership (UK/USA)

- Corporation/Public Limited Company (USA/UK)

Naming your business is a hard enough decision, but it is nothing compared to deciding upon the legal identity and status of your business.

Luckily, it is possible to alter the status of a business at any time (with some provisos!), but it is always best to choose wisely, and think long-term in the first place. The status of a business can bring 'status' …

Becoming CEO of a PLC does sound great, but floating a company is not always best for your business and it's going to be very difficult to get potential shareholders interested in a company that has yet to begin trading!

Choose wisely and ensure that you remain in control.

It is important to note that as a civil law jurisdiction, many of the entity types available in the USA, although they share similar names, differ considerably from those of common law jurisdictions such as the UK.

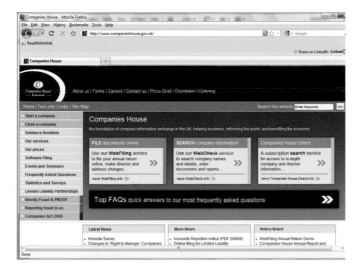

Don't forget

Find an accountant sooner rather than later – they can help advise you on the best option.

The three main types of entity available in the United States are corporations, limited liability companies, and limited partnerships.

These entity types are attractive to both residents of the United States of America wishing to conduct business locally and nationally, and to international entrepreneurs seeking to develop a business presence in the United States of America, or to use the jurisdiction as part of an international offshore strategy.

For residents conducting business locally in the USA, it is generally advisable to form an entity in their own state, for national or international businesses or investors, unless there is a compelling reason to do otherwise, the states of Delaware and Nevada should be strongly considered as these states offer certain advantages. It is strongly advised you seek professional assistance when creating a company in any country.

Legal Structures

Sole Trader

A sole trader is (meant in the nicest possible way) the bottom rung of the status ladder. And with that comes quite a few benefits and a few disadvantages, but most importantly it speaks volumes about the perceived 'size' of your business, which can work both for and against you. A sole trader has unlimited liability and so is responsible for all the debts of the business. However, more and more large firms are happy to deal with sole traders because they appreciate the risk that the individual is taking and feel they are more likely to get a good service and value for money.

There are advantages to running a business as a sole trader – you do not need to inform Companies House about the business, simply register with HMRC as self-employed and you're ready to start trading.

Limited Liability Company

The Limited Company or Limited Liability Company is often regarded as the best thing that the Victorians ever did for us. A limited company is regarded as a completely separate legal entity from those that run or work for the company (thus the directors have limited liability) and with that definition comes a number of benefits and disadvantages.

By creating a limited company you can give the impression of size and experience very easily, even if the business is completely new. Customers will be happier to pay invoices issued by suchandsuch Ltd. than by Jon Smith. However, some suppliers are less keen for small companies to be limited because it can give the impression that you are protecting yourself from risk, which ironically makes you a risky bet. Banks tend to feel the same and in a bid to ensure that any money they lend to a business is in some way protected or secured, will ask the directors to sign a mandate ensuring that if the business is unable to meet repayments, you as director/s will. Filing accounts with Companies House is a legal requirement if you become a director of a limited company and there are knock-on costs if you require your accountant to prepare these documents for you.

Hot tip

You can choose to be sole trader initially and then register as a limited company in the future.

Beware

Read up on your legal responsibilities as a director first before rushing in.

38

Partnership / Limited Liability Partnership

A partnership works for a number of industries and types of businesses exceptionally well, and not so well for others. The classic examples of partnerships are law firms and accountancy firms. With a standard partnership the partners have unlimited liability and this means you would be liable for the business debts of your partner/s even if you were unaware of their debt. There are however tax advantages to forming a partnership. A recent invention is the limited liability partnership, which is almost a fusion of partnership and limited company in that the partners enjoy the protection of limited liability but remain partners rather than directors.

Don't forget

For a limited company you will need at least one additional director – choose someone sensible.

Corporation / PLC

It's highly unlikely that you will form a PLC or Corporation at the start up stage – not least because it's going to be hard to find shareholders to invest in just an idea. Going public is often seen as the king of the status pile – publicly owned immediately conjures images of size and access to capital, even though the truth of the matter may be far different. PLC's work very well for creating a buzz and interest in your (well, actually, not yours anymore!) company, but with the extra cash raised from the flotation and shareholders, comes your commitment to being scrutinized and having to appease shareholder sentiment and need for return, sometimes over longevity. It is paramount to understand that shareholders own PLCs not the directors of the business. You could be voted off the board but equally you could be CEO of multi-million dollar international conglomerate far quicker than through running a partnership or limited company.

Choosing A Company Name

The name of the company does not have to be the same as your business website domain name, it's entirely up to you.

Reasons to operate under the same company name/domain name:

- Some business owners prefer one single name because it's simply easier to convey to staff and clients who is providing the service

- Customers will be invoiced/billed by a company with the same name as the service provider

- Your headed paper, invoices and documentation have one clear name, one clear brand

Reasons to operate under a separate company name/domain name:

- The online business you are creating could be one of many

- If your service or product offering is diverse, you may wish to create a separate brand/website for each

- You may want to deliberately separate your online business offering from an offline service

Beware

Check the name you want hasn't already been taken by searching on the Companies House website.

40

If your online business is operating under a different name from your company name you must make this clear in your terms and conditions and invoices/receipts with an explanatory sentence such as: Convert247 is a trading name of Agasba Ltd, registered in England and Wales company number: 04391356, VAT number: GB 98170956

Social Enterprise

Social Enterprise Schemes seem to be this year's black – it seems every organization is more giving, green or generous than the next. Is this just an underhand marketing technique, a guilt-laden waste of time, resources and money, or is it a strong business philosophy that proves beneficial not just to the recipients but to the organization and the staff that work towards it?

Done right, a social enterprise scheme or social commitment from a business works on so many levels and can contribute to the success of your business in many tangible ways:

Marketing: I'm not suggesting for a minute that you adopt a Social Enterprise Scheme merely for the kudos and marketing/PR opportunities, although without doubt a strong commitment to local community, charitable organizations or green issues certainly garner more free press inches than a boring, sales-message-heavy press release.

Staff Retention: Your existing and potential staff members are all individuals who have interests outside the workplace and the marketplace. They go home to their local communities and to a greater or lesser degree they are affected by social issues that impact them, their families and their wider communities – or to look at it another way, the people and places our business ultimately depend on; the staff and the customers. Therefore, if we as business owners can support these concerns, be actively involved and involve our staff, this philanthropic activity gives staff an additional reason to work and remain motivated over and above the desire to earn a salary. Likewise, staff considering working for an organization may feel motivated to apply for roles at your organization if you are actively involved in Social Enterprise Schemes that they feel strongly about.

Tax benefits and breaks: Depending on which country or territory your company is registered in, there are fiscal benefits to Social Enterprise Schemes which can of course make a difference to your bottom line.

Financing Your Business

Your new online business will cost money to set up. Whatever it is you want to do and even if you will be developing the website or application yourself, you will require the services, products and skills of other people and other companies. If you are planning to sell products, then you will require opening stock as well as suitable packaging materials. Whatever your business, you will need to market your enterprise and have suitable communication tools in place to make and receive calls, send and receive emails and host and maintain a website through which customers can interact with your service. A successful business means a financially successful business and this boils down to making more money than you spend. The bad news is, at least initially, you will have to spend some money before you can earn money. This means your business will require start up funding and investment.

Beware

Undervaluing your own personal financial needs can jeopardize the business.

The good news is that there are a number of financing options available to new e-business owners, and it's sometimes possible to combine a number of financing sources to ensure you have sufficient funds to get started through to break even and profitability.

The cardinal sin of many start-ups is to underestimate how much money will be needed to get the venture operational and into profitability or to budget correctly for your own or your staff's remuneration. Poor financial preparation will scupper even the best online business ideas and it's of critical importance that you get your numbers right and make sure you have the cash in place to give your online business every chance of success. Here are some of the avenues you can explore to raise funds:

Personal Savings

Your own savings should be your first port of call in terms of raising finance – the money has already been acquired and taxes paid, you don't need to ask anybody for it and crucially there will be no monthly repayments, interest or sharing of equity involved. You will need sufficient funds to finance your venture – not just the capital costs of setting up the business, and marketing the site, but enough to be able to support yourself for the first 9 – 18 months during the time your business is growing, but not necessarily in profit or paying you a full salary.

For many entrepreneurs this means remaining in employment whilst they plan and launch the business, using savings to cover the set up costs but being able to feed, clothe and house yourself with funds from another source – i.e. your salary.

For other entrepreneurs, either through circumstance (i.e. redundancy/dismissal) or by design, this new start up venture is their full time role and they plan to dedicate every working hour to getting it to market.

There is no right or wrong way of starting a business – your own personal circumstances will dictate how you proceed. Of course, if you're working full time on a project you will get to market quicker and will have time to dedicate to the business and to steer towards profitability.

Without doubt laying your savings on the line is of course a risk and you could of course lose it all. If you're nervous about investing your own money, unsure of whether the idea 'is good enough' then maybe it's time to revisit your business plan before you spend a penny – if you can't convince yourself of the merits and potential of you and your business, you'll have a hard time convincing investors.

...cont'd

Friends And Family

If you don't have the funds required in your own savings account, the first port of call for many entrepreneurs is their friends and family. Few of us are blessed with extremely rich benefactors happy to lavish six figures on your latest business venture. Far from it – that money was hard-earned and represents your friend's or family member's future, so they're not going to fritter it away.

There are strong arguments in your favor when attempting to raise money from friends and family:

- Friends and family know you, know your work ethic and are aware of your past failures and successes. That shared history is a positive working in your favour

- Each of us is looking for ways to invest varying amounts of savings so that we can enjoy a return on our investment. Unless your family members are completely risk-averse, they will be interested enough at least to hear you out, read your plan and assess the merits of investment

- Standard-issue savings accounts offer savers next to no return on their money – investing in new businesses or the stock market is seen as a viable alternative

- Friends and family may or may not end up investing financially, but pitching to them is great practice for you in terms of understanding and 'selling' your business and making your friends and family aware of your project builds your first potential customer base, can start word of mouth marketing and gives you access to free (sometimes welcome, sometimes not) advice

Beware

Friends may want to invest to help you out – make sure they can comfortably afford to.

When approaching friends and family about your business, you must treat them the same way as you would an external investor. They will need to know:

- What you are planning to do and how well you've planned

- The business is in safe hands

- What their money is going to be used for

- What are the expected returns

- When they can expect a return

- What is expected of them other than 'cash'

- The risks

Any agreement you reach between friends and family must be clearly recorded. There's no free lunch and as with any investor, you will have to agree on the amount to be invested and what this entitles the investor to receive in return – i.e. an equity share, profit share, a position on the board, shareholder rights and responsibilities etc.

Note that although it may be clearly written in your agreement, by nature of the fact that friends and family know you, should they decide to invest, the cash will come with varying amounts of additional 'advice'. With a financial interest in your business, friends and family are often more 'interested' than you would like and to varying degrees may expect some say in the management of the business, or the marketing or may just want to 'chat' to you about how things are going. All the time...

Don't forget

Any one who invests in your business must be kept informed of progress.

45

Banks

Banks are an accessible way to raise finance.

Bank finance usually comes in the form of a bank loan and/or an overdraft facility on your business account.

Bank finance in the form of a loan or an overdraft is usually cheaper than selling shares or equity in your business, and importantly, for many entrepreneurs, leaves you 100% of the equity and therefore 100% of the control.

Approaching Banks

As with any investor, banks want to know that their money is in good hands and will be used for legitimate business purposes. A business plan is an essential requirement and expect to be quizzed about your numbers – especially revenue estimates and your costs.

Banks have lots of experience of investing in small or new businesses and will see through over-inflated or inadequate estimations.

Dress To Impress

You may be starting an online business, and plan to do most of the work, certainly initially, dressed in your pyjamas at the kitchen table – that's fine, in fact you'd be hard pushed to find a suit-wearing internet company… However, you're asking a bank to invest in you and your new business and rightly or wrongly your business manager is going to judge the validity of your business idea based on your business plan and you. Look the part, play the part and dress to impress.

Using Your Bank

As we explored in Chapter 1, help is around, if we ask. Your assigned business manager may not be familiar with the intricacies of your particular niche market, but working in the business community they will know other service providers who may be of use to you – accountants and lawyers for example. If you're unsure of a calculation or want some advice regarding your business plan, ask to speak to someone at the bank. Like you, banks want and need new customers, and therefore need to 'sell' themselves to you. The bank that proves the most helpful, will likely secure your ongoing banking requirements.

Hot tip

Shop around for the best deal – look for free banking at least for the first 12 months.

Beware

Check the fine print – compare interest rates carefully.

Essential Facilities

Even if you plan to finance the business yourself, or with the help of friends and do not require a bank loan or an overdraft facility, be sure that these services are available with your particular account. Overdrafts are not the cheapest form of cash, but having the facility in place from the start, just in case, is much more prudent (and cheaper) than accidentally going into the red.

Bank Loans

Banks are very cautious about who and what they invest in. As a business they need to ensure that the money they lend will be returned. Banks, therefore, will usually insist on a guarantee before lending a new business money. In some cases this requires the company officers to personally guarantee the loan repayments. Even if the money is being borrowed by a limited company, the liability is therefore placed with the directors to make good the repayments should the business falter.

Banks also want to see that theirs is not the only money being risked on the new venture, and will be much more forthcoming if they can see that you are personally investing funds, or that you've secured funds from other sources. Many banks will insist on matching funds, which means they will lend you the equivalent of what you are providing yourself.

Be very wary of loans that are secured on your personal property such as a car or a house – make sure you fully comprehend the impact of losing these items will have on your life.

Don't forget

Insist on a business account with Internet access to save time and money.

47

Grants

Depending on your industry or location your business could benefit from government or university funding.

It's highly unlikely you'll qualify for either government or university funding assistance if your business is essentially an e-commerce store or service provider aimed at the general public and employing 3rd level educated staff. However, that's not to say that it's impossible if you're prepared to open a distribution center in an economically deprived area, or actively recruit staff from a particular socioeconomic background.

Opportunities are limited, competition is fierce and any grant allocation will come with a number of caveats and strict rules which must be adhered to, but if there's a grant available, and your business fits the criteria, not only is the cash useful, but any partnership with government (be it local, state or federal) or with a University adds value to your business and can sometimes include additional assistance in the form of consultancy, joint ventures or a route to interns, new graduates and the latest technologies or research papers.

University

Rightly or wrongly, Universities are diversifying from their core activity of education and now need to be run as, and act as, businesses. Many universities offer spin-off or spin-out business incubation programs for staff and students and also need to partner with external businesses to fully exploit and utilize their innovation or IP.

Government

To encourage innovation or to help drive investment into a particular area or community, the government often offers specific grants to try to assist new or growing businesses. Government grant money of course requires an often long application process and you may not be successful.

Search the web for available schemes that relate to your business model, product or service offering. If you qualify, the application process itself is useful for your business not only for you to perfect your business plan, offering and presentation skills, but also the additional exposure it offers.

UK: www.grantsnet.co.uk　　**USA**: www.sba.gov

Enterprise Finance Loan

Previously known as the Small Firms Loan Guarantee, the Enterprise Finance Guarantee is a government-backed scheme available in the UK. Should you be facing difficulty raising finance because you can't provide suitable security for a commercial bank loan, this scheme could provide the answer.

The Guarantee is to lenders (i.e. banks) and covers 75% of the lenders' exposure on individual loans to small or medium sized businesses. The guarantee covers loans from £1,000 to £1 million and covers most business sectors.

The lending bank will make the ultimate decision on whether to lend the money to you, but with the government providing security through their guarantee this can sway their decision. Obviously, as with any loan, you must adequately demonstrate your ability to pay back the money.

More information is available from www.bis.gov.uk

The Business Link website summarizes the criteria of the scheme as follows:

- There is a guarantee to the lender covering 75 per cent of the loan amount. The borrower pays a premium of 2 per cent per annum on the outstanding balance of the loan, payable to BIS

- It is available to qualifying UK businesses with an annual turnover of up to £25 million

- It is available to businesses in most sectors and for most business purposes, although there are some restrictions

- The lender is entitled to seek unsupported personal guarantees but is not permitted to take a direct charge over a principal private residence for a new Enterprise Finance Guarantee loan

Get it while you can!

Don't forget

If you do receive a grant, mention it on your website, it shows others trust in your business.

Projecting Income

It is not an exact science, but very quickly you will need to determine how many customers you can expect per day, month and year and how much each of them will spend on your products and services. Although nobody is expecting absolute accuracy, very few people will be fooled by sheer hope...

Picking numbers out of the sky is one sure way to complete your projections quickly – but the document will be useless.

Being True To Yourself And The Business

In some respects you can get away with sticking a pin in the tail of the donkey and coming up with any old figures to present in your business plan – but the only person that you will be deceiving is yourself. You will never project figures completely accurately, but better to take an educated guess, based on hard facts and research that you have conducted, than to just make them up.

A huge mistake is to view both the creation of the business plan and the financial statements as a chore that you need to complete for someone else's benefit. Primarily they are both documents that you need to create for yourself and revise religiously; other people will need to see them along the way – but the primary audience is you, and the best business plans will be referred to again and again.

These documents should become the benchmark by which you judge yourself, not abandoned files that are demoted to the third drawer of your filing cabinet. They will act as anchors to stop you veering off on a particular tangent and they will be a great indicator as to whether things are going as well as they should be.

If it turns out, very quickly, that the figures you have projected have become either unachievable or desperately under actual performance, then you can alter your future projections accordingly.

Get out of the mind set that your projected sales are merely figures you need to create in order to secure finance and get the project off to a start. They are your future and the more accurately you can predict future success, the more chance you have of securing the finance that you require in the first place; and making your business a resounding success.

Market Share

If the data exists, then you will quickly be able to determine from Internet sites and paid-for research how large a market you are intending to enter.

A great starting point, although one which we all run the risk of trying to over-achieve within, is how much of the market you intend to command after 12/24/36 months of operations. By determining market share, you already have a fiscal value associated with the market worth, and therefore, your percentage of the market also equates to a financial value.

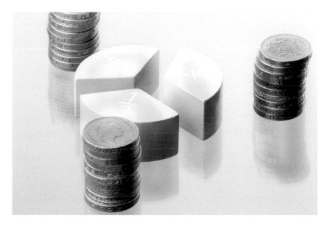

When creating your financial spreadsheet, you can break that figure into the number of customers required and the average customer spend. Bingo – not an exact science, but you now have a baseline figure with which to work. This is how much you feel is achievable; these are the number of customers you need/expect to buy from you, and this is how much they will be spending…easy isn't it?

No. Your financial figures need to be cross-referenced with the time it will take you to get up to speed, allow for the competition to raise their game and for there to be a sudden depression in the market – how would it affect your particular line of business, if interest rates suddenly sky-rocketed and consumer confidence was shattered? Would you be the first or last industry to feel the pinch? All valid questions which need to be considered. Already you have moved beyond the point of just guessing wildly about what numbers to include in your projections.

Business Angels

Business Angels are private investors who wish to invest in start up or growing companies by investing, more often than not, their own funds. Many Angels have themselves made money through running and eventually selling successful businesses and this investment route allows them to keep a hand in business (usually in a market sector they're experienced with) and to seek a healthy return on their investment.

Hot tip

Look for Angels who have enjoyed success selling similar products or services.

52

Most Business Angels invest in companies looking to raise between £10,000 and £250,000. Many Angels will only invest in the areas where they possess expertise.

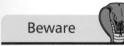

Beware

Anyone with cash can declare themselves an Angel – look for value added experience.

Remember that accepting Angel investment means more than receiving cash – with a vested interest in the success of your business, the Angel will open their contacts up to you, you're also getting a sounding board to bounce ideas off as well as an industry expert who's been in your shoes, succeeded and is looking to do it all over again, through you. Angel partnerships, when they work, work really well.

Equity investment, be it through an Angel or a Venture Capital fund, is an ideal solution for those businesses that do not want to increase their level of borrowing, or are unable to provide the necessary security.

As the old maxim states, it's better to own a percentage of something than 100% of nothing. Or to give you an example, with your own limited funding in place let's say your business grows in year one to be worth $100,000. With an equity investment partner you could say grow your business to be worth $500,000. OK, so now you have 60% of the business instead of 100%, but that 60%, in this example, is worth three times more.

Venture Capitalists

Regarded as the 'serious end' of business venture financing, seeking venture capital is a complex discipline which requires hard work, preparation, intimate knowledge of your business, market and financials and above all else, TIME.

With the best will in the world, seeking venture capital is not for the faint-hearted – you and your business plan will be stretched, assessed, turned upside down and shaken vigorously. This process is known as due diligence and may well leave you exhausted but if successful, you will have raised significant funding (usually >£1,000,000), gained a board member or two, have access to advice and assistance from experienced investors, and although you will have relinquished considerable equity in the business, you've now got the team and backing in place to grow.

Don't forget

VCs like to see the model proven – get your website live and secure early orders or customers first.

Where To Find Venture Capitalists

The web is a great place to start your search for potential venture capital funding. Research the funds, understand what kind of businesses and industries (or geographic area) they're interested in and at what stage they prefer to invest – start up, growth funding etc.

In the UK try:

www.bvca.co.uk/home

In the US try:

www.vfinance.com

Projecting Expenditure

How long's a piece of string? The answer to this question will be unique for every single new online business. Your budget has to be honest, well thought out and clear. Sufficient funds to cover your capital expense, website hosting and maintenance and a realistic amount for you, the business owner. Whether you are working on this project full time with no other income stream, or whether you are launching the business whilst remaining in employment will alter this figure drastically.

Setting up an online shop through which you sell a physical product, will no doubt mean a budget for opening stock, packing materials, shelving and unless you're utilizing a bedroom or garage, a suitable premises to store the products. If you're planning on providing a service, then your costs will be greatly reduced but marketing your company and your services will still need adequate investment. You need to budget not just for staff requirements, but sourcing those staff members is an expensive business.

Hot tip

Beg, borrow or steal office essentials before paying retail price – you don't have to buy new.

Beware

Costs mount up quickly – the more accurate your research, the less likely you'll be surprised.

...cont'd

The important factor to remember is that being realistic about your financial needs is absolutely critical to the success of your online business – hedging your bets and hoping that if you ask for less, you'll be more likely to get it, is short-termism that can cripple your business and can actively contribute to the failure of your business, before you've even started.

Shrewd, honest, detailed financial planning is the order of the day and every hour you spend preparing and testing your numbers is helping to lay the very solid foundations you will need for your business to succeed.

Budgeting and financial forecasting is never a task that is ever truly completed. Your forecasts are only good before you start trading – once the first real sales arrive and once you've paid all the actual invoices you've received, you need to adjust your forecasts accordingly.

For the purpose of your business plan, it's impossible to provide absolutely accurate costs but what you can do, with research, interaction with suppliers and a pen and paper (or more likely a spreadsheet program) is provide accurate expenditure forecasts.

The following should help:

- Website Design/Development & Hosting
- Stock
- Packing & Shipping
- Administration/Customer Services/Sales/Marketing Staff
- Online and Offline Marketing
- Accounting & Book-keeping
- Insurance
- Vehicles, Communications & Tools for business
- Plant and Machinery

Presenting Numbers

Many of us fear numbers, or see working on spreadsheets as a terrible chore, but working accurately with spreadsheets will quickly show you, and others, if a business is viable. Present your financial data accurately to help you realize your ambitions…

These financial documents can be a prophetic vision of your financial future; when the hard graft is over each month, those figures you have entered under salary will be your reward. Not bad for having an idea….

Future Proof

When first creating your financial spreadsheet, you really should be looking to prepare for every possible eventuality that you can foresee over the next three years. Create the row that acknowledges each and every route to market, service offering or product range, even if you are projecting sales to be 0 for the first year. Include everything like bank interest rates for loans and overdrafts, even if you are self-funding the business at launch – you may have a bank loan in the future and it is much easier to alter the rate of interest and enter an amount that you will be paying every month than it is to create a new spreadsheet.

A Picture Says A Thousand Words…

Presenting the data can be done by simply printing off a copy of the spreadsheet – but very few people (apart from maybe an accountant) will be happy with this document. Once the numbers are inputted, use the software you are employing to create more viewer-friendly versions and excerpts of the data. Visually, graphs help readers 'picture' and understand the data far easier than looking at an enormous spreadsheet. Although the viewer might need to refer back to the source document, your message can be displayed very quickly and accurately with a graph. Likewise, in your business plan you want to be summarizing the data with simple one-line statements of fact or intent e.g. with £47,000 investment we intend to create a business turning over £390,000 with a net profit of £61,000 within our first twelve months of operations.

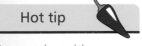

Hot tip

Have a play with your spreadsheet program – a simple click of the mouse can create great graphs.

Beware

Content is always more important than presentation – function first, form second.

Cashflow

When presenting data it is imperative to show when cash is actually going in and out of the business. If the rent bill is £12,000 per annum, display the outgoing funds, broken up into payments, as they will occur (most likely quarterly or six monthly payments) not forgetting to account for deposits and legal fees if applicable. Managing cash flow will be the key to making your business a success.

Find out what terms your suppliers offer, and always try to negotiate more favorable terms. Suppliers are often wary of new businesses – and rightly so, as so many go out of business leaving big debts unpaid. Some suppliers will demand a pro-forma payment for your first order (usually your largest, because you are buying in your opening stock and often want to show a broad range), which only adds to the expense of a new business getting off the ground. No matter how good your negotiation skills, some suppliers will demand a year of good relations before allowing more generous terms, or for the value of orders to exceed a certain level.

Don't forget

Not all of your customers will pay on time, allow some contingency for late receipts.

	A B	AA	AB	AC	AD	AE	AF	AG	AH	AI	AJ	AK	AL	AM	AN
1	ESTABLISHMENT														
2	Rent & service charge	4,000	4,000	4,000	4,000	4,000	4,000	4,000	4,000	4,000	4,000	4,000	4,000		
3	Web-site costs / server	1,200	0	0	0	0	0	0	0	0	0	0	0		
4	Utilities	500	500	500	500	500	500	500	500	500	500	500	500		
5	Cleaning	300	300	300	300	300	300	300	300	300	300	300	300		
6	TOTAL	6,000	4,800	4,800	4,800	4,800	4,800	4,800	4,800	4,800	4,800	4,800	4,800		
7															
8	COMMUNICATIONS														
9	Telephone & fax	1,000	1,000	1,000	1,000	1,000	1,000	1,000	1,000	1,000	1,000	1,000	1,000		
10	Company Postage	300	300	300	300	300	300	300	300	300	300	300	300		
11	Internet connection/s	400	400	400	400	400	400	400	400	400	400	400	400		
12	TOTAL	1,700	1,700	1,700	1,700	1,700	1,700	1,700	1,700	1,700	1,700	1,700	1,700		
13															
14	ADMINISTRATION														
15	Staff training / recruiting	400	400	400	400	400	400	400	400	400	400	400	400		
16	Insurance	1,000	0	0	0	0	0	0	0	0	0	0	0		
17	Sundries	600	600	600	600	600	600	600	600	600	600	600	600		
18	Offline marketing	1,000	1,000	1,000	1,000	1,000	1,000	1,000	1,000	1,000	1,000	1,000	1,000		
19	Online marketing	4,925	5,417	5,959	6,555	7,210	7,932	8,725	9,597	10,557	11,613	12,774	14,051		
20	Shows and Exhibitions	0	0	0	0	0	5,000	0	0	0	0	0	0		
21	Legal & professional	0	1,000	0	0	0	0	0	1,000	0	0	0	0		
22	Bank charges	300	300	300	300	300	300	300	300	300	300	300	300		
23	TOTAL	8,225	8,717	8,259	8,855	9,510	15,232	11,025	12,897	12,857	13,913	15,074	16,351		

Fundraising Is Tough

Raising finance doesn't always go the way you'd hoped; the general economy plays a huge part, along with investor inertia during particular moments in time.

Thanks, But No Thanks...

When you have a great idea for a business, it is often quite difficult to understand why everyone is very happy to talk to you about it, shows excitement about the opportunity and truly wants the idea to succeed, until you mention that it needs some funding. Suddenly instead of an empty hat going round and hands digging deep into pockets, there is an awkward silence and people make their excuses and leave. Don't lose heart, positive feedback about your idea or your business plan is valuable, even if it doesn't raise the funds you need.

More Self-Funding

It may amount to very little, or it may amount to quite a lot, but it is important to exhaust your own means of raising cash before asking for any more from anyone else. Quite simply the more you borrow from others the more you will have to pay back, and the more control over your business you will lose. If you can reduce that amount by even hundreds of pounds or dollars, do it.

Do not sell yourself short and pretend that if you sell the car to raise money, you can always buy another one, once the company gets started – No. This won't happen and you will be without a car for a long, long time. Instead, look to raise money by selling off unused items you own, whether it be old CDs, DVDs or furniture. Many of us own tons of extra stuff we do not use, sitting in boxes in our own or, worse, other people's houses. Make these items work for you and sell them. There are of course the traditional routes such as a car-boot or garage sale but with the glut of online auction houses and Amazon's marketplace program, you can start selling without even lifting a finger – well, maybe one to left-click your mouse – but it's all very easy and the money is paid straight into your bank account.

Cash will make or break your business – getting your hands on to as much of it as you possibly can, is your goal, but you may need to re-work your business plan to reflect a lower investment which may mean launching the business with less of a product or service range, or targeting a smaller niche – and then using the funds from the business to bankroll the growth.

Hot tip

Rejection isn't the end of the world, listen to feedback, revise your plan, try again.

Beware

Promises of funding are one thing, but don't celebrate until the money's in your account.

Paying Yourself?

It's highly likely that you are launching your new online business to support yourself financially as well as satisfy other desires such as your work/life balance, showcase for your skills and 'being your own boss'. Although launching a new business assumes, and often demands, that you suffer a period of austerity and belt-tightening, it's absolutely essential that you are clear in your own mind and within the business plan, what you plan to take out of the business each month, and that amount is sufficient for your needs.

How Much Should You Pay Yourself?

We'd all like to earn enough money that would ensure no more personal debt, numerous foreign holidays per year and the ability to save towards a new house, boat or tropical island... In the meantime, there's the real world. Everyone's circumstances are different, but if you haven't done so already work out your own personal and family expenditure. What is the minimum you require each month in order to cover your commitments? Be conservative but be honest.

How Do Investors View Your Salary?

Whether you're seeking funding from a bank, a Business Angel or friends and family, they will be very aware of your basic need for a salary. In fact, the absence of a proposed salary will be conspicuous. A realistic monthly stipend shows you are planning to run your business as a professional entity that rewards labour. Granted, your initial salary won't be as generous as what you might be worth in the employment market, but that's part of the deal when you run your own business – obviously the more successful your business is in the future, the larger your salary can become.

Conversely, proposing a high salary for yourself, and then presenting your business plan, cap in hand to investors, is not going to go down too well. Investors want to see their money spent on capital expenditure that directly impacts the growth of the business and ensures a return on their money – keeping you in the lap of luxury isn't a great ROI.

Chapter Summary

- Write the business plan primarily for yourself, not for potential investors – it's your guide to launching and running your business

- Any third-party assistance you pay for now, such as assistance setting up a company, hiring an accountant or legal advice, is money well spent to ensure your business is built on solid foundations

- Research your proposed market. Pay attention to your competitors and find ways that you can do the same, but better

- Plan an exit strategy for the business – maybe this is many years in the future, but will allow you to focus on where you want to be in 3, 5 or even 10 years time

- Get to grips with your numbers. There are some essential documents you need to be able to create and more importantly understand. Start with a P&L Account and The Balance Sheet

- There are many ways to finance a business. Choose which combination works best for you and your company. Weigh up the pros and cons of selling or sharing equity

- Explore any grant options that may be open to your business, from government or universities

- When projecting both future income and expenditure the more research you conduct, the more accurate your projections

- Cashflow!

- Ensure your business plan includes a realistic remuneration plan for yourself… not too much, not too little

3 Setting Up Online

With your business plan written, it's time to put the wheels in motion. This chapter explores the steps you need to take to move from offline idea, to online business.

Getting Online

Everyone knows somebody who can create a website – developers are ten to the penny as they say; but will they be able to deliver what you want?

It is no good asking a team of developers to build you an online business without giving them a brief of what you want, when you want it and how much you've got to spend. We all have our own ideas about how things should work and how things should look (and how much things should cost) so, with the best will in the world, if you don't tell the developers what you want, you won't get it.

Before contacting a developer or agency about your business, can you answer these questions? Do you even know what it is you want from your website? How many products or services will you offer? Will you want to regularly change the appearance, layout and functionality of your site? Who are you trying to target with the website? Which features are essential for launch, and which features will you want to introduce further down the line?

Developers won't expect you to provide a full technical specification, but they will require a brief which they can convert into a fully-functioning website. Providing a copy of your business plan isn't good enough, nor is a 2 hour presentation with you animatedly describing your business model… what you need is a bullet point list, which the developer can work from so that you'll both be happy with the end results.

Hot tip

Spend a day online – take notes, compare features, designs and even colors.

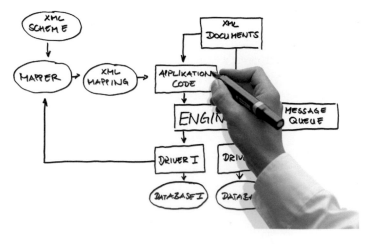

To get you started, have a think and write down the answers to the following:

- **How many pages?** Look at your competitors or at websites you admire. Don't worry too much about product pages (these will be dynamically created) what you need to work out is the number of static pages such as 'Contact Us', 'About Us', 'Privacy Policy' etc. List the pages and you'll be halfway to creating a sitemap.

- **Content & Structure** – Do you want to display just text and images? Are you planning to include lots of rich media such as video clips, downloads, blogs, customer reviews etc? This will help the developer to decide on the most suitable technology for the website.

- **Content Management** – Whatever your product or service, you'll want to add/modify/delete content from the website. Giving the developer an indication of how much of that content will need to be modified, how often and by whom, will allow them to create a Content Management System (CMS) that delivers.

- **Marketing Plans** – be sure to read Chapter 6 before answering this question, but if you have an idea of which on- and offline marketing channels you plan to exploit with the business, your developer will be able to build in functionality that will allow this to happen, on launch or in the future. It's far easier to build the functionality to handle discount vouchers from the start than add it in the future. If you're going to be using Search Engine Marketing such as Google Adwords, you'll need a selection of Landing Pages and if you'd like to accept payments in Euros, Pounds and Dollars, your developer needs to know!

- **Back Offices and Reporting** – You'll want to know how well your website is performing in terms of visitors, conversions, bounce rates and where your traffic is coming from. Ensure your developer is aware of tools such as Google Analytics and integrates this into the website. If you're planning an e-commerce store, you'll also want more detailed financial reporting – not just the number of sales, but tools to manage returns, stock levels, Sales Tax/VAT and pricing.

Choosing A Partner

When deciding on a web development partner to help you launch your online business it's important to research a number of key factors before making a decision. Use the following top ten decision influencers:

Experience

If you had the skills, you'd be doing this yourself. As you don't, you're willing to pay a professional to provide a service – make sure they are professional and they're going to provide the service you've requested on time, to specification and to budget. Assess how long the web developer or agency has been operating and what types of online projects they have worked on. There are infinite website designs available but the clever money would go with a developer who has experience working with clients who sell similar products or services to you as they have already been through the learning curve and understand your target market.

An experienced developer will be able to talk to you about technology options and the pros and cons of each and be very wary if there's no mention of best industry practice, accessibility and usability in any of your phone call or email exchanges.

Web Development Skills and Knowledge

You are paying a professional to deliver a much better product than one you could create yourself. It is therefore imperative that you determine the skill set your chosen developer or agency can provide to your business and how it complements your own – ask them about their views on HTML coding and CSS best practices. Whether their code is W3C compliant and whether the site will be multi-browser compliant? Will the website be scalable, allowing the addition of extra pages or features in the future? Do they build the website from scratch or use a template? If you're planning to sell products online then you'll need to assess their e-commerce/shopping basket solutions, knowledge of payment gateways so that you can accept credit cards etc. and for any website, some form of Content Management System that will allow you or your staff to add/edit/delete information on the website.

Hot tip

Insist potential developers provide a portfolio you can verify.

Website/Client Portfolio

A website developer should always provide a portfolio of work completed. An image says a thousand words, and if you don't like the style of the sites they've delivered, negotiations are probably not going to begin. Note that the design of any website is a collaborative effort between the developer and the client, and so the developer may have been designing to order. Be sure to look at their full portfolio as it may be you like elements from a range of sites which, when merged together, are exactly what you are looking for.

References From Clients

A business owner should be proud of their work and therefore, shouldn't balk at the suggestion that you would like to talk to one or more previous clients. Your development expense will be one of the major early investments you make, and can quite literally make or break your business. Apply the same rigorous vetting procedure to your potential developers as you would to a potential employee.

...cont'd

Project Management

A website build requires intricate planning, attention to detail, collaboration with the business owner, and strict project management control, especially of budget, time and resources. Ensure that your chosen development company explains how the process will work; how often you can expect to be kept informed about the project, who are your contacts and how you can reach them. If you're happy with remote collaboration, say so, likewise, if you'd prefer one-to-one on-site meetings specify this. Never forget that you're the paying client and your chosen developer or agency should put your wishes above all else.

Availability, Workload & Commitment

You will have a date in mind for launch, once this is communicated to your developer and a launch schedule is agreed upon you will need commitments that this date will be honored. Partly this will be through the project management tools mentioned above, but should also be reflected in the payment terms and schedule you agree with the developer.

Hot tip

Share your research with your developer – you're much more likely to get what you want first time.

Beware

Allow sufficient time to find a development partner – don't rush the decision.

Flexibility

No matter how detailed your planning there may well be a new feature or an alteration that has to be made to the website due to changes in the market, new legal legislation or a change of direction for the business – ensure that there is some contingency in the developer's time scale to allow for this. Note that changes that are additional to the original specification will affect your developer's budget and the time line, and both you and your chosen agency need to be flexible.

Location, Location, Location

Although physical location shouldn't be an issue in the digital world, it can be. Face-to-face meetings aren't always necessary but can prove invaluable at the point of selecting a development partner and ongoing throughout the build and beyond. Depending on the complexity of your project and your own preference for face-to-face meetings as opposed to electronic communication, you may do well to select a developer who is physically close to you. Obviously with the suite of tools available to business owners, including email, video conferencing, VoIP services such as Skype, it's more and more common to hire a developer in a different city, if not country…

Education/Qualifications

Many developers teach themselves aspects of their profession – new techniques, code and even entirely new programming languages. Some studied formally and some just picked it up. Equally we've all met people with fantastic formal qualifications who have absolutely no idea how to operate in the real world…

A developer's portfolio and recommendations are your strongest indication of their abilities, if that can be backed up with industry-related qualifications, you've found yourself a really strong candidate.

Personality

Judging someone on how they appear to you (both physically and through their communications) might seem to be somewhat superficial, but you're not just employing someone to build a website – you're entrusting them to create the foundations of your online business. If you don't like the way they conduct themselves, communicate to you through their website, on the telephone or through email, it's as good a reason as any to choose someone else. The effort they place on marketing and selling themselves to win your business speaks volumes about how much attention and focus they will place on your project.

Secure Sockets Layer (SSL)

If you're planning to capture client data or take payments via your website, you have a legal responsibility to protect your customer's data from prying eyes.

Regular internet connections between client and server (i.e. your PC and any http website) such as when you surf the web for the latest news, sports or browse at your favorite online shoe shop, or when you send or receive email, or utilize one of the many instant messaging services such as MSN, AIM, Yahoo! etc – all of these actions take place over unsecured connections, which means that the information you transmit can be viewed and stored by a third party.

A Secure Sockets Layer is protection from these prying eyes and provides a safe way for client and server to communicate.

SSL protocol encrypts the data being sent across the internet between the client (you) and the server (the website you're visiting) which renders it useless to any prying third party.

SSL In Action

You know your connection to a website is secure when you see the web address begin https:// and on some browsers you will notice a closed padlock icon.

Your developer will be able to add a Secure Sockets Layer to your website without difficulty, prices have plummeted recently and it's even possible to get an SSL certificate for free. Branded SSL certificates from companies such as Verisign cost between $200-$800 depending on the level of security required and additional features.

Ordinarily, the vast majority of your website will be accessed via http, allowing users to browse your services and products. The switch to https happens when a user wants to log in to their account, or pay for items in their shopping basket.

As part of your on-site marketing it is very important to highlight that you employ SSL on your website, customers will feel more secure conducting business through your site and confident passing on their personal data and payment details.

Payment Solutions

The most important aspect of any e-commerce website, whatever product or service you are providing, is the payment solution – allowing you to charge customers online.

To enable online payments you will need to set up a payment gateway and a merchant account.

Payment gateways are an interface between your website, or more accurately your server, and banks/card issuers around the world.

Hot tip

Competition is fierce between providers, so shop around for the best payment solution.

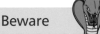

Beware

The application process for a payment gateway takes time – start early.

A search for [payment gateway] or [payment solutions] will return a huge selection of providers. You can choose to work with a specialist provider, your own bank or another bank. Ask for quotes from a selection of the above and compare set up fees, monthly fees and the percentage charge per transaction. Ideally, you want to choose a partner who is sympathetic to your status as a start up and will allow you to scale quickly. Most providers work on a scale, so the more transactions you conduct a month, the cheaper the per-transaction fee will be.

Merchant accounts are a depository (usually a bank account) into which the funds you receive from online payments are paid. This account is separate from your company bank account. Although you may well set up your merchant account with your existing business bank, it is not obligatory.

How Does It Work?

Whichever payment gateway you choose, fundamentally the process works as follows:

 Payment Card Data Collection – The customer enters their card details on your website.

2 **Payment Card Authentication** – Those details are sent via your payment gateway, (i.e. RBS Worldpay, Sagepay, VeriFone) to the card issuer (i.e. the customer's bank). If the card details cannot be verified, the payment is normally declined and your customer is asked to check their details are correct, or use an alternative card.

3 **Payment Authorization** – The issuing bank checks the cardholder's details are correct, that there are enough funds in the account to cover the payment and that the card hasn't been reported lost or stolen. If the details are all correct, the issuing bank authorizes the amount requested and reserves those funds. Once the payment transaction is complete, a final instruction is sent to the bank to debit the funds.

4 **Payment Settlement** – Your merchant account is credited with the value of the card transaction within a few days of the actual transaction.

Alternative Payment Types

In addition to, or as an alternative to processing customer credit or debit cards online, there are a huge variety of payment options available which can be added to your website without the need for merchant accounts, long term contracts or monthly fees.

Hot tip

Offer customers a variety of payment methods, your stats will soon tell you what's popular.

Arguably the most popular is PayPal, which allows customers to pay for products or services without revealing their card details. PayPal integration is very straightforward for any developer and for new online businesses it provides a simple, trusted payment solution and is particularly suitable if you're unsure of your sales volumes during the first few months of operations.

Other payment solutions to consider include Google Checkout, NoChex and Xoom.

Managing Content

In Chapter 6, Marketing Your Online Business, we'll look at creating fantastic content in much greater detail as it plays such a fundamental role in any online business. However, whatever content is created, the process of writing, editing and storing content needs to be carefully managed.

Pre-Launch Content

Every static page of your website, for example [About Us] or [Contact Us] needs to be written. Writing content takes a lot longer than many business owners imagine and you'd be well advised to begin content creation at the same time as you plan the business. Writing content as it will appear on the website helps formulate your ideas and sharpen your message.

If you're not a natural writer, have difficulty expressing ideas in words, or struggle with the rules of grammar, employ outside help – your website is your shop window and customers will make their purchase decision based on the information you present to them – although a pretty product image will help, written content is king.

A Second Set Of Eyes

No matter how skilled you are with words, every writer makes mistakes – in fact, the more pages of content you write the more mistakes creep in. Professional writers have editors, and you should too – make sure every single snippet of text has been read through by someone else before it's committed to your website. An error or two will always be forgiven, but it jars with the reader, and plants doubt about your website's professionalism and knowledge.

Unique Content

Unique content plays a big role in effective Search Engine Optimization (see Chapter 6) but creating unique content is about creating a company identity. Copying and pasting content from a selection of other websites is not a solution – your website will become a mixture of different voices which will confuse the reader, i.e. your potential customer. By all means research competitor websites to understand their approach, but ensure you or your content writer creates fresh text that is particular to your brand and online business.

Don't forget

Regularly back up your content files on a pen drive and/or server.

Managing Images

Imagery plays a massive role on websites, and therefore should be an essential part of your design and product or service offering. Although your web developer will know how to present images to maximum effect they can only present what you provide them with. Therefore, it's as important to source good quality images that will help sell your business and products or service as it is to write exciting text.

Manufacturer Assistance

Manufacturers, generally, produce and provide images of their products for use by retailers. This is fantastic if you're planning to sell their products on your website. Ask for image files early in the relationship so that you or your developers can work with the images and optimize them for use on the website. If possible, ask for both hi- and lo-res versions of the images so that the same images can be used on- and offline, should they be required.

Creating Your Own

Unless you've got the equipment and the skills, taking your own product images for use on an e-commerce store is a risky move – you don't want your site to look like a series of eBay listings, with the product resting against your bedroom wall, or presented on your kitchen table…Not only is the visual impact of your images important, it is essential that you ensure that the images are maximized for use on the Internet. For once, the best is not necessarily the most ideal. The quality of an image (assuming that it is a good photo, or design in the first place) is determined by the pixel size and the number of pixels to be shown per inch (dots per inch or dpi). When preparing images for printed material, the rule of thumb is to save the image with at least 300 (if not more) dots per inch. When you are altering images to be shown on a website you must reduce the dpi to 72.

Hot tip

Ask your developer about including a zoom function on your website for product images.

Image Libraries

Royalty-free image libraries make the life of designers and website owners very easy indeed. The business models differ slightly but whether it's a pay-as-you-go or a subscription-based model, essentially you pay a fee for each image you require. The image is royalty-free, meaning that you pay once but can then use the image on your website without further cost. Image libraries generally include accurate search and filter functions allowing you to search for specific themes, or styles to get the image/s you require.

Don't forget

If you decide to use a professional, timetable some shots of yourself for PR and Marketing.

Image Database

Your developer will look after the image database for your website, but as a business owner, be sure to have a back-up of your images just as you do for your website text content. Images are generally large files, so an external server or hard-drive is more advisable than a pen-drive or removable media.

Labeling Images

There are conflicting schools of thought regarding the labeling of images. As a business owner it's essential that you employ a naming convention that works for you, so that you can find the image you want, when you want it. However, as a general rule, including pertinent information in the filename of an image, such as a unique product name, identifying code such as EAN (barcode) or the people or scene portrayed in the image, not only makes it easier to find the image in your own database, but impacts Search Engine Optimization far more than calling an image something like: DCIM248330078.jpg

The Order Pipeline

Despite your future efforts to market your website and attract new visitors to the site and your efforts to ensure the right products are available at the right price – if it all goes wrong at the end and users find it difficult to actually buy from you, then it is all in vain…

Working with your developer, here's how to ensure that the ordering process is problem-free for the customer and you don't let them leave without spending some money!

Hot tip

You only need one customer phone number – don't ask for mobile, home and office.

Keep It Simple

The act of a user placing an item into their shopping basket and the consumer's path to purchase is often referred to as the order pipeline. This is the process and number of pages a consumer must navigate before their choice/s of purchase become their own. Just as good web design is all about offering both simplicity and usability; an effective order pipeline is equally short and to the point. If you had to complete an obstacle course every time you wanted to conduct your weekly grocery shop, you would soon look to another supermarket that was far easier to navigate and give them your custom. The same is true for websites.

Just The Essentials

When designing your order pipeline look to shave off as many stages as possible between a user selecting what they want to buy and the order confirmation/thank you page.

You need to define which details are essential for this order and what information can be captured at a later date. Put simply, the longer the process, the fewer customers who complete their purchase. You can lose as much as 50% of customers who've placed an item in their basket for every page of the order pipeline.

So, if one hundred people put an item into their basket and there are five pages of order pipeline, you could be looking at just over three orders actually being completed. Imagine the difference if you had only 3 pages – you could be enjoying over twelve orders per one hundred instead of just three...

Managing The Customer Experience

No matter how slick your order pipeline, customers like to know what's going on – there can be a delay when your server is awaiting a response from your payment gateway that the customer's card details are correct.

Although you cannot speed this process up, you can let your consumers know what is happening, and even if it is as simple as showing a sand timer or a message – explain that the site is still working, just looking for information from another source.

Likewise it is probably worth your while to offer a phone number and a fax number for people to leave their credit card details – although the fear has gone from most web users about the safety of their card details, there still exist some users who feel safer reading their card number to a human being and not entering their details online. You are quite within your rights to charge a surcharge to cover the associated administration costs.

Most importantly to lose a customer at the purchase page can be avoided if you provide a phone number – whatever their difficulty you can answer the call, and hopefully save the sale. No number, no sale.

Don't forget

Make the order process as straightforward as possible.

Brand Management

In Chapter 6, Marketing Your Online Business, we'll look at creating your brand in terms of messaging, positioning and tone; but managing your brand isn't so much a marketing function as it is an executive function that should be at the core of your strategy from pre-launch to beyond…

A Strong Logo

Web branding is an absolute necessity. Whether you are a large corporation or an individual – like it or loathe it logos are essential – in some cases the brand becomes bigger than the message it represents.

When creating a logo, think long, hard and carefully about your decision. A logo in the real world will hopefully be an instantaneous visual image that is synonymous with your company. This is no different on the web. The best example is e-commerce operations that not only brand their site, but reinforce the message with branded packaging materials – ensuring that not only the end-user but everyone who has anything to do with the delivery of that product is aware of the company (and to an extent the product/s contained within). A logo should be visually stunning, attention-grabbing and to an extent self-explanatory.

www.longcomplicatedname.com

There is a lot to be said for having a short snappy web address. Not only does it roll off the tongue better, it allows less room for error on the part of the user. Every letter is a potential spelling mistake, and every spelling mistake is a potential lost customer.

Don't feel that your domain name has to be a proper name, or anything vaguely related to the name of the company behind it. This is all about marketing, exposure and design. If a made up word makes some sort of sense, won't win you a triple-point-score in Scrabble and when you mention it to people they know immediately how to spell it – you're on to a winner. It's increasingly hard to find available domain names due to the increase of speculative domain purchases by domain parkers and profiteers. But seek, and you shall find.

Beware

Make sure you can register both the .co.uk and .com domain name for your business.

Google Alerts

Google provides a wonderful free service known as Google Alerts which can be found at www.google.com/alerts. You can enter a search term or phrase you are interested in tracking and decide on the frequency of updates, i.e. once a day, through which you will be notified of new references on the web to your phrases of interest. As well as creating an alert for your business name, create additional alerts for your industry, product range, service offering and even your main competitors. This daily or weekly digest provides untold amounts of competitor information, ideas for articles or pages you could write for your own website and an overview of how and by whom your key phrases of interest are being used on the web. Set up your business name alert prelaunch and you'll also be able to spot the moment that pages of your site are indexed by Google.

Don't forget

Once you've decided on a company name, register the name on the social networks.

Twitter Search

Twitter whether you like it or loathe it has an accurate pulse of what's hot and what's not at any given time, use Twitter Search to understand whether your brand, area of interest, products, services or competitors are being mentioned. Twitter Search shows you which users are talking about your topics and through your own Twitter account, you can follow these users and create not only a list of potential customers, but partners, content providers and future brand evangelists.

Online Business Essentials

Every business is unique and will therefore have specific requirements, however, there are some essentials that transcend every industry, and if you're going to be operating online, you'll need the following to a greater or lesser extent:

Hardware Requirements

PC/Mac/Notebook – it doesn't have to be the absolute top of the range, but you'll want a fast-performing machine that can handle you running multiple applications simultaneously. Early business planning will require at least a word processor and spreadsheet package, but as time moves on, the applications will become more complicated and the need to be able to view and manipulate images, work with large amounts of data and manage large databases of products and customers.

External Storage

Back up everything – from the first draft of your business plan right through to launch and beyond; get in to the habit of making copies. Of everything. Hardware fails, more often than manufacturers (and users!) would like, and the loss of data can be catastrophic for your business, whatever stage you're at. Thankfully, technology advances every year and a high capacity external hard drive or space on a server can be acquired for minimum investment. Don't limit your backup to text documents; you'll need to protect your site images, product data, site code and databases.

Printer/s

High quality printers have become very affordable and offer a new business owner the opportunity to produce high-quality documents for internal and external use. No matter how much we pretend we're moving toward a paper-less office, it simply isn't true, your business will have numerous documentation requirements, drafts, meeting agendas, and once you're launched invoices, receipts and packing slips require a professional printing solution, not the basic printer you received free with your PC!

Hot tip

Before buying any software, search on the web for open source versions that do the job.

Monitor

Working with a web-based product, it's essential you are viewing your own website and those of your competitors through a high-quality monitor. If you prefer to work from a laptop, invest in an external monitor for use in the office (or your kitchen table) to ensure that graphically, your website, products and marketing material are the best they can be.

Scanner

For e-commerce stores especially, a scanner is a key piece of kit allowing you access to additional art work that may be paper based, and will prove it's worth in terms of recording essential paperwork critical to running your business. Digitizing important company registration documents, VAT or tax documentation is just the start...

Digital Camera

A good quality camera will prove invaluable for most online businesses – buy the best you can afford and be sure to keep it on hand. Images of your offices and staff will prove useful for your website and to include in press releases etc.

Software

We all have our preferences regarding software, either from familiarity or due to our choice of operating system. Some online business essentials include:

Adobe Photoshop, for photo manipulation, Dreamweaver, for HTML manipulation, if you're inexperienced with the language, and Acrobat, so that you can create PDF documents (either to include as downloads on your website, or to send clients proposals), etc. Being web-based it's essential to test your website across all the major browsers, even if you personally prefer to use one over the rest. Be sure to download Firefox, Internet Explorer, Safari and Chrome.

And for UK-based businesses, if you're looking for a free entry-level accounting package, take a look at: www.tassoftware.co.uk.

For Project Management purposes – MS Project is pretty comprehensive, but if you're looking for a free open source tool check out Gantt Project at: www.ganttproject.biz.

Don't forget

You don't have to buy everything at once, stagger purchases as required.

Chapter Summary

- Research potential development partners; quiz them on their skills, background and previous clients

- Document the features you want from your website; your developer will be able to provide a more accurate quote and deliver to your expectations

- Study your competitors' websites for ideas – especially features, look & feel and general tone

- A Content Management System is essential for your online business – you must have the ability to add, modify or delete pages of content, products or services by yourself

- If you're planning to capture private customer data through your website, such as personal details, order details or credit card payments, you will require an SSL certificate

- Shop around for the best payment solution for your business. Offer your customers a choice of acceptable payment methods

- Your website content, be it text, graphics or images is the very essence of an online business, ensure you are using the highest quality and make copies

- Manage your brand from the outset with free tools such as Google Alerts and Twitter Search

- Ensure you have the right tools, software and applications to do your job and manage your website's many pages

4 Monetizing Your Site

There are a variety of ways to make money online. Many successful websites choose to capitalize on a combination of revenue streams. This chapter explores some of the routes you can take to monetize your site.

Selling Online

There are a variety of ways to monetize your website, and importantly they are not mutually exclusive; many sites combine a number of monetization routes to maximise the value of the traffic they receive on their own website and through affiliation, thus earning revenue from sending their traffic to other websites.

What begins as a secondary revenue source, such as offering advertising on your site, with the right amount and right type of traffic, can become your primary revenue source.

Decide which model works for your business and always keep an open mind regarding opportunities for additional revenue streams, now and in the future.

Selling Physical Products Online

Business to Consumer (B2C) e-commerce is the most common business model adopted by new online businesses. This includes the selling of products you buy from a manufacturer or supplier and re-sell to consumers, or products that you create or build yourself, such as pieces of sculpture, paintings or jewelry. Whatever the product, this is a classic offline retail model, transferred online.

Depending on your industry, depending on your product range and depending on from where you acquire your stock, will all influence your costs. This product acquisition cost therefore plays a massive role in helping you decide upon the final price you offer to consumers – the retail price.

Selling Digital Products Online

As the availability, acceptance and appetite for digital products has grown, so too have the number of online stores selling them. Digital products such as ebooks, music files, video downloads, software (downloads or boxed products) or digital information such as market research have exploded over the past few years and the market shows no sign of abating.

As with physical products there is always a cost associated with product acquisition, be it a license or re-seller fee, or in the case of selling your own software or ebooks, the cost of development of the product/s.

Pricing Strategy

When deciding on a pricing strategy, be sure to allow for any applicable taxes such as Sales Tax/VAT, any discounts you may want to apply to customers (now or in the future), the cost of customer acquisition, including any marketing costs such as banner adverts or Paid Search (PPC) and a further allowance for initiatives such as referral schemes, affiliation commissions and cashback programs. You will also have to allow for the cost of packaging and postage/courier rates in the case of sending physical products and factor in either your own time or the cost of a staff member to physically pick and pack the order. On top of all that, if you're processing a customer's credit or debit card online, then no matter which payment provider you partner with, there will be costs associated with each transaction such as monthly fees and a percentage of transaction value charge.

Don't forget

Run a variety of pricing strategies through a spreadsheet program to see what can work.

Of course there are economies of scale to be achieved when you start selling in large volumes, but in the early days of any start up, selling products online can prove very expensive. By the time everyone else has taken their share of the sale price, there's sometimes very little left for you!

Your competition also plays a huge role in influencing your pricing strategy – you will have decided upon a price point through which your business is to be positioned – in simple terms, either you want to be one of the cheapest, somewhere in the middle, or one of the most exclusive. Other than opting for exclusivity and charging whatever you like, your brand positioning will limit the amount you can charge customers, meaning that margins will likely be very tight.

Membership/Subscriptions

A very interesting and often cost-effective way of operating online is through the provision of membership or subscriptions.

Software providers have seen the appeal of a regular monthly fee over charging a one-off fee. From a customer point-of-view the monthly fee appears more economical than a large one-off fee; the promise of free upgrades whilst subscribed allays any fears of product redundancy and the flexibility to cancel the arrangement sits well with sceptical consumers. From the business's point-of-view, the monthly charge model is great for cash flow, provides up-selling opportunities and capitalizes on Customer Relationship Management through the minimal monthly contact.

Online gaming sites (such as Massive Multi-player Online Games), dating websites, specialist information and specialist social networking sites all follow a similar model. There is of course a cost to creating content and acquiring members/users, but the value of the business is the network and once that has grown, it can be a cash cow that keeps on giving.

With subscription or membership-based services business owners are often faced with a chicken or egg conundrum. What comes first? A large customer or user base which in turn justifies a monthly charge or charging first, and hoping the customers pay...

A neat tactic is to create a buzz and find your core customer base by discounting or even offering access for free, initially. Granted this tactic is not great for your cash flow, but will allow you to build an initial base who can then hopefully be charged at a later date if they continue to require and like your product or service offering. Similar to the Freemium model of offering a 'taste' of a product first and then encouraging users to upgrade to the paid version at a later date, can work very well indeed.

Don't forget

Good content is worth paying for – if your content is value added, consider charging for it.

The Pay Wall

Without word-of-mouth, extensive PR, reviews or a general buzz about your product or service, it is very difficult to convince customers to pay for something if it's not exactly clear what they are getting for their money. With established large online newspapers, for example, it's a reasonable assumption that paying for the content hidden behind a pay wall will result in access to quality articles.

As a new business potential customers do not have that trust or knowledge of you and your service and therefore, it's essential to tease your users with examples. A great example of this is dating websites which allow limited access, such as viewing five profiles, but turn off features such as contact details, until you pay the fee.

Showing users what's contained behind a pay wall is essential if you want them to put their hands in the pocket, but think long and hard about how much information you release, and when.

Price Elasticity

You're free to charge whatever you think the market will pay for a subscription or membership to your services. Unlike fixed-price products however, users are much more sensitive to price changes once they have engaged with your service. It is much advisable to research your pricing well, before launch, than constantly altering your advertised prices as this confuses potential users and angers existing users. Tiers of membership level often work well, if appropriate to your business, with some sort of basic, medium and advanced advantages.

AdSense/Display Advertising

Opting to display advertising on your website is a great way to earn revenue – users of your website see the advertising and if they like what they see, they click. Each click earns you money. Or, every time you show the advert to one thousand users, you get paid.

For advertising programs to work, you must have traffic. You only get paid when users click on the ads, so the more users you can show the ad to, the more likely you will get clicks and therefore cash.

There is a school of thought that argues advertising, even the simple text-based AdSense Program ads from Google can 'cheapen' your website.

Because you want the ads to be seen and clicked it makes the most sense to give the ads pride of place on your web pages which can distract users from the core content of your site.

Granted, if your monetization strategy is to drive as many users to your website as possible so that they can click ads, then great, but if you're trying to create a sticky site; then advertising can work against you.

Extreme display advertising:

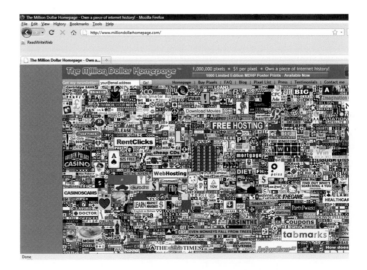

Hot tip

Look at your competitors, how do they approach advertising?

High-traffic websites are attractive to advertisers and the bigger advertising brands and the bigger payouts will be offered to those high-traffic sites willing to offer advertising and that drive significant traffic to the advertisers' pages.

Signing up with Google's AdSense program is very straightforward, as is integration onto your site. You can use Google's back office tools to select the type of advertising you'd like to show on your site, and the adverts that are shown are of course relevant to your website. If for example you have a page relating to travel in Russia, the adverts displayed will be in some way related to this theme (the targeting isn't absolutely perfect, so you will occasionally see some strange associations).

Display or Advertising Banners – often use the CPC (cost per click) or CPM (cost per thousand views) model. Some brands are happy to pay, simply for the exposure and some are looking for leads or sales. Most advertisers are looking for a combination of all three.

There is always a difficult decision to make when you operate an online business and rely on, or require, advertising revenue. Where to place the advertising? On one hand if you're going to try to earn advertising dollars, you want to maximise your traffic's exposure to ads, but conversely, if the first or only thing your user sees is ads, you run the risk that they're going to surf elsewhere in the future and that they'll ignore your core offering.

Don't Confuse...

Advertising could be your route to riches, but to successfully create and build your brand, it's important to position your business and your website in a professional light and if you're serious about selling a product online which you distribute yourself, there seems little sense in also showing adverts for competitors who do the same thing...

Don't forget

Potential display advertising revenue is usually measured in pennies per click!

A Balancing Act

Finding The Right Balance

The balance of advertising revenue versus selling physical and/or digital products, subscriptions or memberships will be something you specify and model in your business plan.

If you are reliant solely on advertising dollars, then of course adverts should be placed prominently on the website and the design of the site should be such that it actively encourages your users to click.

If, like many businesses advertising is a secondary revenue stream, or a temporary revenue stream, then your core product or service offering should take precedence and advertising although prominent should not dominate.

Assuming you wish to display advertising then depending on the complexity of your website, how deeply you want to manage advertisers and the type of advertisers, you will opt for an ad-serving solution such as Google AdSense, an affiliation network such as TradeDoubler, or you will work with selected advertisers direct and add their banner or creative to your website e.g. for 90 days.

Try It, You Might Like It...

If you're unsure, give it a go. If it proves to generate little or no income, a quick change to your website, and it's removed. Advertising will always be a love/hate topic for website owners, but as a new business, any income you can generate through your website is welcome...

Selling 3rd Party Products

The web offers a wide array of revenue streams, and there's a strong possibility you may wish to monetize your site through a variety of these channels.

Even if your core business is service provision, for example providing specialist business services or consultancy and you'd prefer to shy away from display advertising or selling physical products, there exist a plethora of digital products you can promote via your site.

Organizations such as ClickBank www.clickbank.com could be a solution:

● Clickbank has over 10,000 products you can promote

● Commissions are on a scale, offering up to 75% per sale

● Opportunity to earn recurring revenue from subscription-based products

● Full back-office stats to measure ROI and campaign management

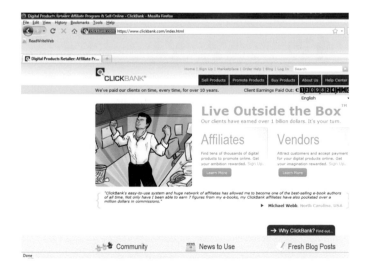

Affiliation (As A Publisher)

Affiliation is a multi-billion dollar industry, encompassing every possible product or service category you can think of.

Affiliation is easy to implement both as an advertiser (those who want others to help them sell their product or service, by paying a commission) and as a publisher (those who want to help sell the products and services of others, to earn a commission) and it can be a very quick way to make money online and never even have to process a single order or provide a service yourself – essentially you are a traffic aggregator for your chosen affiliate partner/s and you make money earning a commission every time one of your visitors clicks on a link, fills in a form or interacts with your advertiser's site, through your site.

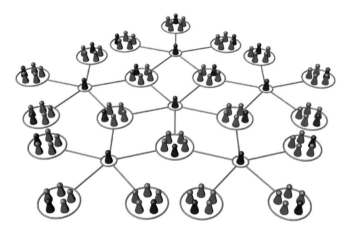

Beware

Search online for discussions about a Network's reputation.

Confused? Let's look at an example, Amazon provides an affiliation service which it calls Amazon Associates:

Anyone with a website or a blog can become an Associate. Once you've registered you are able to access tracking codes, banners, search boxes and tools to add to your website and actively promote Amazon and its enormous product range.

Payout percentages vary depending on the product and the volume of business you create, but in the example below, anyone who buys one of the books on the page below:

earns the Associate (in this instance, me) a healthy 8% of the total value of the customer's shopping basket – I get a commission for the sale of my book, and, a smaller commission from the value of whatever else that customer buys at the same time. Not bad.

This is great if you want to promote the products Amazon sells, but what if you want a range of products or services, or you don't want to work with a single provider and like to keep your options open?

In this case you need to turn to an Affiliation Network.

Affiliate Networks

Where there's a gap, there's a solution. Affiliate Networks are big business – matching advertisers (the companies selling or providing the products or services) with publishers (websites that want to promote other company's products or services).

A search for [affiliate network] plus any particular industry, product type, or service type will show you the vast range of affiliate networks currently operating.

As an online business owner you can choose to become an advertiser (we'll explore becoming an Advertiser in Chapter 6) or a publisher, and it's even possible to be both.

Affiliate networks vary in size, reputation and ability in attracting the 'best' or highest profile advertisers and publishers. The more successful networks will charge advertisers a set up fee to join the program and more often than not a monthly fee for managing the account. Conversely it's usually free to become a publisher, and that's why it can prove to be a lucrative secondary revenue stream for your business, or even a primary revenue stream. Affiliate Networks make their money from the set up and monthly fees paid by advertisers along with a commission (sometimes as high as 30%) of the total revenue generated for the client.

Hot tip

Networks tend to grow by channel – i.e. one will be better for Health, another for Books.

Becoming A Publisher

Let's say you're interested in selling lingerie online. It is quite possible to run a successful business selling hundreds of orders a month without once ever buying or selling your own stock. You don't need to ship any orders and you don't have to process any card payments or deal with customer service issues… this is possible through affiliation.

How?

Banners – at the 'entry level' of affiliation is the option to place advertiser banners on your website – these can be simple text links, search boxes or larger banners and images that you add to your site along with appropriate content – for example an article about the latest shoe fashions with a corresponding mention and image of an advertiser's website. If your website visitor clicks on the link, and buys a product (even if the actual purchase occurs up to 30 days after the initial click through) then you earn a commission – usually a percentage of the sale price. By incorporating advertiser banners on your site, you can promote an unlimited amount of advertisers and earn revenue every time there's a purchase that originated from your website.

A great example of this practice at work:

Don't forget

If you like the idea of affiliation, there's nothing stopping you setting up more websites.

This website compares dating websites – the website owner writes a review of each of the services and provides a link, it doesn't matter which service her visitor chooses, if they click through and register, she earns a commission.

Product Feeds

At the more 'professional end' of affiliate marketing, is the product feed or XML/CSV feed.

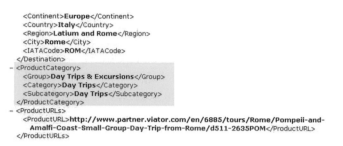

```
            <Continent>Europe</Continent>
            <Country>Italy</Country>
            <Region>Latium and Rome</Region>
            <City>Rome</City>
            <IATACode>ROM</IATACode>
          </Destination>
     − <ProductCategory>
            <Group>Day Trips & Excursions</Group>
            <Category>Day Trips</Category>
            <Subcategory>Day Trips</Subcategory>
          </ProductCategory>
     − <ProductURLs>
            <ProductURL>http://www.partner.viator.com/en/6885/tours/Rome/Pompeii-and-
               Amalfi-Coast-Small-Group-Day-Trip-from-Rome/d511-2635POM</ProductURL>
          </ProductURLs>
```

Hot tip

Product feeds are a great way to promote your product range – check out Chapter 6.

Accepting a product feed from an advertiser can require some development work and API integration, but what this gives you is the ability to display as many or as few products as you wish from an advertiser's website.

For example, maybe you want to promote footwear products; by integrating a feed, your website can display the images, the product names, prices, product descriptions and customer reviews etc.

Your user can browse the products and should they wish to purchase, seamlessly click through to the advertiser's website and buy – earning you a revenue for simply providing the customer.

Below is how an advertiser's feed might appear on your site:

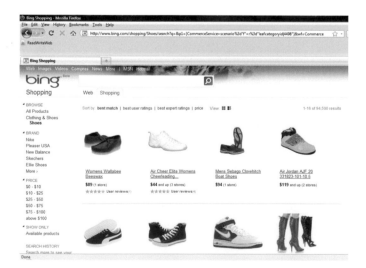

Product Feeds are an incredibly effective way to build a large website, quickly.

Many business owners use feeds as a way to trade online, without having to worry about stock, sending orders or dealing with customers or returns.

It is also an effective way to practice selling a particular product range online, without the risk.

A tactic could be to set up a number of affiliate sites, each selling a different product range on behalf of other retailers, whichever one proves to be the most successful could be the one you choose to work on full time – or maybe, the affiliate sites prove to be successful enough in their own right!

Effective tactics for selling via 3rd party product feeds:

- Ensure your website design is tailored to support the chosen product range – color palette, navigation, and search and filter options must be similar or better than other retailers operating in the same field

- Read the small print very carefully, some advertisers have strict rules on how you can market your website if it includes their products – e.g. not being allowed to bid on certain keywords with Search Engine Marketing – this can be very restrictive

- Add value to the product feed – just displaying verbatim what is provided by the advertiser will not help your Search Engine Optimization nor give customers a good reason to search for products on your site, over the advertiser's own site or a rival affiliate. Additional content such as product reviews, additional product information, images or information will set your website apart

Become An Authority

Becoming an authority is a medium to long-term goal for your website, but one which can prove to be both profitable and effective in building your brand and awareness.

Whatever industry or market you are planning to enter with your new online business, there may or may not exist an organization that seeks and rewards excellence within the industry or that promotes that excellence to the general public.

Hot tip

There's more on becoming an authority site in Chapter 6.

Business To Business

If, for example you are planning to launch a website to promote your accountancy services, why not create a directory which lists other accountants, who look after particular aspects you yourself don't cover, or related businesses that often work alongside the accountancy function, such as legal services? This arrangement can be on a commission or referral basis (possibly even reciprocal).

Taking the concept even further, imagine for a moment an authority site which displayed all the possible niche disciplines of Accountancy, and within each of the categories were listed the top 20 service providers as rated by the authority site. Initially you would create this directory for free (well, at least on a referral basis, rather than charging up front), over time, with traffic increasing you could put each of the listed businesses through a set of rigorous assessments – references from verified previous clients, etc. Over time, you have an accurate profile of each and a recognized and trusted ranking system.

...cont'd

By limiting the places to say 20 per niche category, businesses would have to pay to retain their spot. There are examples on the web of industry directories which charge as much as $1000 per month per category. With a range of niche categories and as many as 20 or 50 businesses per category, it's a great way to earn extra revenue through your website.

Business To Consumer

On the business-to-consumer side, if you sell health and beauty products, why not create an award for each beauty category, e.g. best hair care product. The first time round you simply issue the awards – i.e. best hair care product – to the winners, based on your own viewpoint. You'll have to alert the manufacturer and maybe add a winner's logo on the product detail page of your site. The next time round, you could query your customer base, on the website, or via email marketing, so that they can vote on their favorites. Over time, the manufacturers include you in new product releases, ask for reviews and strive to win future awards.

Get noticed by your industry and by customers interested in your products or services by making yourself an authority website that others look to becoming a part of.

Chapter Summary

- Selling products online can be done without ever having to stock or ship a single item – affiliate marketing offers the opportunity to great commissions for forwarding customers

- Think long and hard about how you price your products or services – where does that position you in terms of the competition? If you're high end, you'll need to make sure that everything from the look and feel of the website right through to the quality of your packing materials all support that pricing structure

- Advertising can provide a great revenue stream for your website, but it only works if you've got traffic

- Memberships or subscriptions are great for cash flow, if you've got something of value on offer, charge for it; but give users a taste before you ask them to buy…

- Consider product feeds for truly effective affiliate marketing and the highest affiliate payouts, but add to the information to set your website apart from the competition

- Think outside the box and set your website apart from the competition by becoming the authority for your product or service; this can lead to a valuable revenue stream

5 Supply Chain

Running a successful e-commerce business requires a website that works. But behind the scenes, lies the true heart of the operation – the supply chain. This chapter explores what you need to do to get your products from manufacturer to consumer...

Buying Local

If you can find a local supplier of the products you wish to sell online, then this is hugely advantageous to your business.

Local means green – if the products don't have to travel far between supplier and retailer then of course you are reducing the impact your business has on the environment in terms of fuel consumption and emissions.

Local means reduced costs – using a local supplier will affect your bottom line – reduced shipping costs, free local delivery or self-service pick up options all mean less money spent getting the product into your storeroom or warehouse.

Local means better stock management – forging relationships with local suppliers can lead to added benefits for your business – suppliers might agree to hold stock on consignment, which means they hold it for you but you don't pay for it until you sell it. They might be able to agree to reserving stock, meaning you carry the bare minimum at your own premises, and top up when you need to easily, knowing it will be there for you.

Local means marketing opportunities – despite the lure and benefits of globalization, sometimes customers want something else. Your customers are informed adults who often care about green issues, product miles, providence and supporting local business… if you do stock products that are local or regional, say so.

Buying From Further Afield

Prices from South America or South East Asia can be very attractive, and certainly if you find the right partners, it can be clever sourcing that skyrockets your online business into profitability. You may or may not be in a position to visit and vet your potential suppliers and if you're doing your buying blind (only through electronic or phone communication) you have to take extra steps to protect yourself and your cash.

There are lots of online b2b trading platforms which all come with their own business model. Many charge businesses to advertise their contact details and to post a description of their products, others charge buyers a membership fee to gain access to the contact details, and some charge a commission on any trades that take place between members through the platform. Take a look at some of the following major players. The sheer number of potential suppliers and products is staggering.

- www.alibaba.com
- www.tradekey.com
- www.globalsources.com
- www.diytrade.com

Don't forget

Investigate with your accountant how buying abroad can impact your tax liability.

103

Suppliers

The internet will play a huge role in most of the research you will conduct when planning and operating your online business. The internet is especially useful for finding suppliers of the products and services you require.

Choosing A Supplier

The research you do, the contacts you make and the promotional material you receive from all the suppliers you contact, is never a waste. You may not decide to work with each and every supplier you come across now. They may not be right for your business, but those suppliers could be perfect sometime in the future. Keep the essential data and contact details and refer back to it periodically as your business grows and your product offering increases.

Managing Suppliers

Keeping good relations with your suppliers is as important as managing your customers. Without your suppliers, you don't have a business – and suppliers include everyone from your web developer, your accountant to your chosen overnight courier. Even if you're paying for their services, you won't always get 100% service and any failing on their behalf has knock-on consequences for your clients, cash flow and success. Don't forget suppliers have the same pressures and concerns about their business – finding clients, paying invoices, managing staff etc. as you do. A supplier is an individual or a group of individuals who are under internal and external pressures to deliver. Managing suppliers successfully is wholly dependent on how well you communicate with them and it is important to establish a great relationship, right from the start.

Placing Your First Order

You're running a new business, and even if you are known personally to the supplier from a previous role or business, chances are your first order will have to be paid for, up front.

Ironically the one time a business could really benefit from generous payment terms is the one time when you won't get them – as a start up. As well-planned as your business is, you're being lumped together with all the other start ups that have been and gone. You're business is a risk and therefore, it's pretty much guaranteed that you'll have to pay for everything, cash-up-front.

The good news is, once you have a history with a supplier, once you've shown you pay for what you order and assuming you have built a good credit rating, then suppliers will become more elastic with their pricing and payment terms. They are established in the marketplace, you're not... once you're on level pegging relationships can and will improve.

When placing your first order, ensure that you double check not just the order contents and price but the essential account information that the supplier is holding on you – your relationship with a supplier probably began when you first made contact asking about their products or services. The person who took that call, or responded to your email, or met you at a trade fair, may or may not have taken down your details correctly. Check your billing address, delivery address, contact number and emails, Company Number/VAT number and payment terms.

Don't forget

Once you've selected your suppliers continue to keep an eye on the market for new players.

105

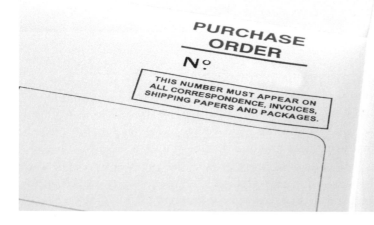

PURCHASE ORDER
Nº
THIS NUMBER MUST APPEAR ON ALL CORRESPONDENCE, INVOICES, SHIPPING PAPERS AND PACKAGES.

Supplier Relations

Assessing Suppliers

When you receive an order, check the contents are what you ordered and the quantities/colors are correct. It's not going to be a great relationship if they have completely messed up your order, but minor mistakes can and do happen to even the best run businesses. If there are mistakes, or items missing, it's important to alert the supplier. Ranting and raging probably isn't going to help, but a clear message that you expect a better service in the future is completely justified.

Conversely, if everything is present and correct, the items are well packaged, the correct documentation is included and the order arrived in good time or on the date arranged, this is great news and you can relax a little bit knowing that you've chosen a professional supplier who values your custom and obviously wants to ensure that you're going to come back.

Hot tip

Make sure you have an account manager – so you know who to call if things go wrong.

Maintaining Relations

A good supplier/client relationship is critical to forging and maintaining a successful business, as we will discover in Chapter 7 Customer Relationship Management. A good supplier doesn't just process your order and deliver the product or service, but seeks to be a 'partner' to your business; keeping you aware of new products and trends in the marketplace, recognizes loyalty, values your custom and never takes you for granted.

If you notice your relations with the organization or more likely a particular member of staff are beginning to fail, it's important to address that with the organization as quickly as possible – if the supplier values their customers they'll look to accommodate your requests to maintain your future business.

Communication should be two-way. As a supplier of a product or service you are using, or have used in the past, then obviously it's in the supplier's interest to contact you via an account manager to keep you informed of what's happening in their world... but think of the difference it could make to your business if you also informed them of what's happening in your world. This can be as simple as providing forecasts for future requirements – giving suppliers notice of future requirements can lead to keener pricing based on bulk purchases and working closely with a supplier can lead to joint venture opportunities or new product offerings because you require or notice a specific niche in the marketplace that answers not just your own needs, but maybe the needs of countless other businesses out there. As you will no doubt do with your customers, build a database of your suppliers. This doesn't have to be any more complex than an Excel spreadsheet, Access file, or even good old-fashioned pen and paper, but make sure that somewhere you have the contact details, essential names and a record of previous correspondence.

Breaking Relations

In an ideal world you will not face this issue as communication and service delivery from each and every one of your suppliers will be excellent... However, in certain cases, despite all of your best efforts, relations with a particular supplier can break down and this leaves your business at risk. If you feel that you're not receiving the best possible service consistently from a supplier (no matter how competitive their pricing) then begin the search for a replacement. Once established, notify your existing supplier that you will no longer be requiring their services and ensure any outstanding invoices are paid, on time. Assuming you made your supplier aware of when things went wrong, your lost custom should come as no great shock if they made no attempt to make the situation right. No matter how great your relationship once was, if the product or service you receive is sub-standard you have to think of your business first.

Don't forget

Above all else, you are the customer – demand excellence.

107

Useful Tools & Gadgets

To run your e-commerce store smoothly, right from day one, you will need to make sure you've got the equipment and tools you need to keep operations running smooth, and ensure that you are presenting a professional front to your customers. Too many new online businesses try to make do with personal equipment that is not up to the task which leaves customers with the impression that you're more of a one-man band, than an established company...

Barcode Printer

Depending on the type of products you are planning to sell, how far up the supply chain you're sourcing your products and the maturity of your particular industry, will determine whether products are provided to you with barcodes. Barcodes make light work of stock management and a barcode printer will prove invaluable if you need to label your products.

Barcode Scanner

To assist you in both receiving (when stock arrives from the supplier) and picking and packing customer orders, a barcode scanner, for the price, will be your best friend. Setting up your back office (even if it's just a simple spreadsheet) will take time as you assign each and every barcode to a specific product, but once done, stock can literally fly in and out of your warehouse as fast as you can pull the trigger.

Hot tip

Many barcode scanners come with basic Stock Management Software.

Beware

Don't print barcodes using an ink jet printer as the codes are likely to smudge.

Stock Management System

Excel works fine for a few line items, but as your stock range increases and volume grows, it becomes more and more unmanageable. Stock Management software ranges in price from less that $100 to the many hundreds of thousands of dollars… Shop around for a solution that fits your needs and your budget.

Talk to your website developers about what they can offer, or recommend, in terms of integration with your website back office. In an ideal world you are looking for a real-time solution which updates availability on the website directly dependent on the actual status of products in your warehouse.

Invoices/Receipts

It is your legal obligation to provide customers with an invoice/receipt along with every order shipped. This invoice must contain your company address and registration/tax details, the specifics of the customer's order and the price they've paid. It's also good practice to include returns information. There are some very clever paper solutions available in which part of the printed sheet (the customer's address for example) is removable and can be used as the shipping label.

You may want to consider purchasing a dedicated laser or thermal printer specifically for processing customer invoices.

Stock & Storage

Depending on the products and the volume you plan to sell via your e-commerce store, will influence greatly the general or specialist equipment you will require for storing your stock. However, there are some basic rules that apply in all cases:

- Stock Care – above all else, it is essential you have somewhere dry, clean and dust-free to store your stock

- Temperature – the warehouse, garage or storeroom must remain at a constant and controllable median temperature. Extremes in terms of cold or heat will damage products and make them unfit for retail

- Protection – ensure your warehouse is adequately protected with fire-prevention equipment, can be securely locked and of course is covered by a suitable insurance policy

- Accurate Receiving – when stock arrives from suppliers, deal with it immediately. Check the correct number of boxes or palettes have arrived and check the contents match the invoice/receipt

- Suitable Shelving – storage solutions aren't cheap, but the investment you make will positively affect the speed in which you are able to receive, store and manage stock. Go for industrial quality and strength

Hot tip

Even if you're operating from home, set up processes you can transfer larger scale.

- Report Discrepancies – there are a number of reasons why you might not receive exactly what you ordered. Stock can be on back order, your supplier sent you the wrong item/s, or the incorrect quantities were included in the shipment. Let your supplier know what has arrived and what hasn't and keep records regarding the level of error. Mistakes can and do happen, but it is how your supplier deals with the problems that will help you decide about using them in the future

- Clear Bin locations – store stock in an ordered and logical way. Have clearly numbered or marked bins where specific stock resides. Once stock has been received, place in the correct bin location and update your stock management system manually or via technology such as barcode readers

- Regular Stock Takes – check the right amount of stock is in the right location at least once a month. This is a task no one enjoys, but failure to do it regularly leaves you exposed to potential problems fulfilling customer orders, and problems with stock loss or theft

Picking & Packing

Enjoying success with your E-commerce enterprise relies on you getting the small details right – and nothing is more important than getting the right product to the right customer. With the best will in the world mistakes can and do happen, but it is your role as business owner to ensure that you have the processes and the tools in place to get customer orders right, first time.

At first you may be able to manage customer orders by yourself, but as demand grows and your time is focussed more on managing the business and less on individual orders, you will need to be sure the following processes are adhered to:

Beware

Packaging materials take up lots of space! Be sure you're able to store them safely and securely.

- Generate picking lists that include the bin location of the products to save time. If you sell products, such as office stationery or clothing and there are different colors of the same product available, be sure that the color, or the color code is clearly marked to assist the picker

- If you offer a gift-wrapping service, allow suitable staff allocation and time to process these orders and ensure you have a suitable and safe working area to wrap

- Ensure the correct invoice/receipt is sent with the correct order

- Double-check the correct items are being sent to the correct customer

- Notify the customer of any items that are missing from the order and when they can expect to receive the item. Give the customer the opportunity to amend or cancel the order in light of the new delivery date

- Ensure items are packaged correctly to withstand their journey. Invest in your packaging material as this is an area where you don't want to cut corners. Damaged products mean customer dissatisfaction and returns... and you will want as few of these as possible

- Recording which staff-member picked and/or packed an order will provide essential business intelligence allowing you to reward excellence and be aware of persistent problems or errors

- Ensure you have the right levels of staff depending on seasonal variations. Staff can always work quicker, but carelessness leads to mistakes. All of your efforts in terms of the website, the content, your product sourcing and your investment mean nothing if you don't get your products out to the customers

Delivery

Customers want their products fast and they also want to receive their items in perfect condition. Delivery proves to be the constant bugbear of online operations – everything about online shopping is about speed, convenience and accuracy… the delivery function is what slows the entire process down and is the area through which most problems occur. Whichever partner you choose, be it a national carrier such as Royal Mail, an international carrier such as FedEx or some combination of private courier and international network, it is at the point of delivery that you are no longer directly in control of the customer experience, and you are wholly reliant upon a third-party.

- Some savings can be made if you pre-sort packages based on their destination address. Each carrier will have different requirements, but negotiate on price if you are able to sort by city/state/country

- Courier companies work on volume and therefore pass on savings to you the more you send. Talk to an account manager about your actual volumes or if you are still to begin trading, your expected monthly volumes and they will suggest an appropriate rate

Hot tip

In the UK Royal Mail offer a reliable and affordable service that will suit most needs.

Beware

Customers are very sensitive to postage charges – pass on savings where you can.

- Look for couriers or carriers who will collect from your premises and even better will specify the time/s of collection

- Some courier companies will also look after your returns with a collection service from the customer's address – this tends to be quite expensive but great for customer service and marketing purposes

- Sending deliveries using branded packaging or branded address labels can be a simple way to increase brand awareness – however, depending on the products you sell, may or may not be suitable. For example if you sell lingerie or health and beauty products, not all of your customers will appreciate 'the world' knowing what's inside the box – this is especially true if the item is being bought as a gift. Branding on packages that contain high ticket values can also encourage theft during the delivery process

- International orders must have a customs statement from your company clearly marked on the exterior of the package which includes a description of the contents such as 'printed material' or 'educational product'. Check with your local Customs office for the exact description covering your product range

  In USA: www.cbp.gov   In UK: www.hmrc.gov.uk

Returns

Despite your efforts to streamline your processes during the pick/pack and delivery phases, sometimes the wrong product is sent to the wrong customer, the product arrives damaged, the courier was unable to deliver to the customer's address, or the customer simply changes their mind about the order and sends it back to you.

Returns are unpleasant for a business owner because it means lost revenue. Depending on the product, the reason for return and the condition in which it's returned may mean you are able to re-sell (as long as it's clearly marked as 'damaged' 'a second' or 'open-box') but generally, you've lost the product, the cost of shipping to the original customer and if you offer a freepost returns address, then the cost of the return postage too.

If you're trading online you will want to do what you can to reduce returns levels and this starts with posting as much information about your products on the website as you can. But even if you avoid any ambiguity in the product description and product images, you will not be able to avoid customers returning items...

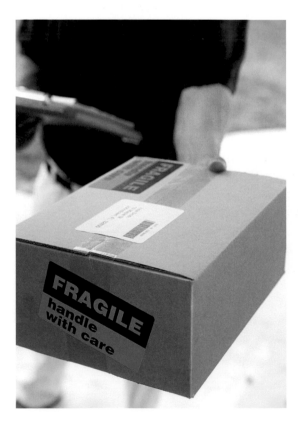

Beware

Check the item returned is in fact a product you sold! Customers can make mistakes too.

- Record-Keeping – Receive returns into your warehouse as you do regular stock from suppliers. By keeping accurate records, you can build up intelligence about returns that may lead to patterns concerning particular products, suppliers, staff-members or customers

- Give Good Customer Service – acknowledge that you have received the returned item/s via email. Process the return based on your customer return policy – i.e. refund the card that paid for the order and send notification to the customer when the refund has been actioned

- Provide a Customer Returns Form – either via your website, or as part of your invoice/receipt. Customers can detail which item is being returned and why they are returning the item. Include common reasons with a check box to speed up the process, such as 'too small', 'doesn't fit', 'not the correct item'. This information can prove invaluable in highlighting which areas of the supply chain are going wrong and give you an indication of what you need to do to address the problems

- Habitual Returns – something that might appear over time is a very small segment of your customer base who return items regularly. This behavior tends to occur more with fashion products and digital products such as DVDs, CDs etc in which the customer simply wants to use the product once and then returns it... Monitor this, but always give customers the benefit of the doubt. In extreme cases you can of course decline to accept orders from a particular email address, physical address or IP Address if you deem a repeated behavior to be unacceptable

Don't forget

Returns are a fact of business life; you can reduce them but never eradicate them.

117

Chapter Summary

- Buy local when you can and make sure your customers know all about it

- Using international suppliers can mean access to great prices and great products

- Ordering from international suppliers adds additional layers of complexity to supplier relations, tax and accounting and lead times – check with your accountant before committing to an international order

- Research your potential suppliers before ordering products

- Spend time building and maintaining good relations with your suppliers

- Know when to patch up a relationship and when to break ranks – your own company must come first

- Manage your supply chain with the help of specialist hardware and software

- Look after your stock, and your stock will look after you

- Care about each and every order you ship and you will reduce your return rates and increase customer satisfaction

- Monitor every aspect of your supply chain. The intelligence you receive will help you become more efficient and save money

6 Marketing Your Online Business

Customers and clients are essential to every business and just having a great website is not enough. You need to market your site so that customers can find it amongst all the other websites selling or promoting similar products and services. This chapter will help you decide which are the best techniques to successfully market your online business.

Offline versus Online

Offline advertising, generally, relies on a scatter gun approach – i.e. if enough people see or hear about your website, a percentage of them will make a purchase or tell their friends.

Although it's certainly possible to target your audience (e.g. advertising your boat hire website address in a boating magazine), you've got no real way of knowing how many people saw the advert and therefore it's difficult to measure your conversion rate.

It is possible to know how many leads it generated if you direct users to a specific landing page e.g.

www.boathire.com/magazinead

But it's not so easy to calculate an accurate return on investment.

Radio and television advertising, although on the decline, is still a firm favorite with some brands partly for its effectiveness and partly for the kudos.

But without doubt, the reason why online advertising has been embraced so categorically, is that everything, I mean *everything*, can be measured, analyzed and accounted for.

...cont'd

Online marketing came into being pretty much straight after the creation of the first commercial websites.

Online business owners needed ways in which they could drive traffic (potential customers) to their website. What started off as posting a link on a simple text-based directory has grown into the multi-billion dollar online marketing industry. Every link, impression, click, registration and sale is trackable, traceable and accountable. This amount of data has made it entirely possible to account for every pound or dollar invested and for business owners to be able to make informed decisions about the effectiveness of their campaigns, almost in real-time. Not just how many leads of sales were generated, but how many eyeballs saw a campaign, which particular advert is more effective, what time of day works best etc.

So which approach should you choose, with your new online business? Well, each business will have its own goals and budget. In an ideal world, if you can afford it, then the simple answer is to invest in both (wisely), but if you're working with limited funds, it's best to work with the techniques that provide the most accurate data so that you can improve or optimize your marketing message and most importantly can accurately control your spending. We'll take a look at your options throughout this chapter.

Search Engines

Most users begin the buying process or funnel (the steps taken between researching a product or service and completing a purchase or contacting a service provider) with a search engine.

The power of search engines to influence a customer's online journey is huge and it is therefore essential that your website is built, maintained and updated to be both customer and search engine friendly. In that order.

Hot tip

Customers acquired through Search Engines are free! Make this channel a priority.

Beware

Search Engine Optimization takes time – don't expect overnight results.

Search Engine Optimization

Good Search Engine Optimization or SEO is not about tricking the Search Engines into ranking your website, it is about making your website visible to the Search Engines, and primarily Google – filling it with relevant and unique content and building up an online reputation that the Search Engines can't possibly ignore.

SEO is a broad topic and deep analysis is beyond the scope of this book. There are many good sources of information available to further your understanding of SEO, however the following advice will set you well on your way to performing well on Search and enjoying qualified and 'free' traffic.

Make Your Website Visible

It might sound too obvious to mention, but you have to be seen to be ranked.

Google employs a piece of software known as the Googlebot to scan individual web pages on the internet and what it finds (or critically, doesn't find) has a direct impact on how thoroughly your website is indexed and therefore how well it can rank in the natural Search Engine Results Pages (SERPs).

Quality Content, Unique To Your Site

An often quoted phrase you may have heard is 'content is king'. It's not wrong. Good content is key to a good website. Good content is attractive to human users because it helps inform, educate, inspire and importantly, sell your product or service. This means more users visit, more users benefit from your content and ultimately more users become consumers of your product or services. Good content is also attractive to other website owners who want to provide relevant, interesting or value-added content to their users; if you've got good content, then they will link to your pages. Good content is also attractive to Google and the other search engines because good content means that Google can supply a suitable solution to their customer's search – a link to your website. But here's the best bit – if Google thinks the content is good (read: accessible, structured and relevant) and other websites think your content is good, and thus link to it… then Google will take into consideration these third-party votes of confidence (links) and the net result is your site ranks higher.

A Reputable Website

A by-product of providing good content on your website (text, images, videos, downloads etc) is that other websites will link to your content. This is great in itself because it positions your website as an authority on your given product or service, it results in more traffic as users of other sites click on the link to consume the content on your pages and it also makes Google sit up and take notice of your web pages resulting in more visits from the Googlebot because your website is regarded as reputable.

Keywords... And Phrases

Don't obsess over highly-competitive single words or phrases in a bid to rank #1 – for starters, cramming in the word "accountant" onto every page of your website in the hope of ranking #1 for the search term [accountant] will not work – Google will see this as keyword stuffing and actually penalize your site. It's far better to study the words and phrases that users actually type in to Google. You can do this through Google's own keyword tool at https://adwords.google.com/

Hot tip

Find your niche keywords and concentrate on writing content to exploit them.

Beware

Write content for customers, not for Google!

For example, data for the term [accountant] reveals that it is indeed a popular search phrase.

Without doubt it's worth creating pages of content that include the term [accountant] but this simple research also shows that by creating additional content that focuses on [accountants], or [accountancy] together with specialist pages containing specific content on say [tax accountants] and [accounting services] your pages will appeal to a much larger amount of search traffic; i.e. those users who are searching for derivatives of the word accountant and words relating to the topic or service.

So you might not achieve the top position for [accountant], but you'll be receiving lots of qualified traffic who are interested in your specific accountancy services, rather than unqualified traffic who may or may not have been looking to hire your firm.

This is how to profit from the long tail of Search; without doubt, the most powerful weapon in online marketing.

...cont'd

<H> Tags

As a rule of thumb, Google likes to be guided as to what you believe is the most important content on each and every webpage. The way to do this is to employ Header or 'H' tags within your HTML. Through your Content Management System defining or adding H tags should be a straightforward process.

H tags are the way you tell the search engines that this 'H', or 'header', is worth paying attention to – it's like making a sentence bold – it gets noticed.

Whilst you may have physically altered the text to be bold, or italic or presented in a larger point size, Google ignores these stylistic alterations as they are merely cosmetic. It's looking for <H> tags, and your job is to tag content in order of relevance and importance in terms of its relation to the rest of the content found on the page. If there are four main focuses to your web page then you're well within your rights to label each new focus, or topic, with an H tag, ideally listed in ranking order – H1, H2, H3 and so on.

To label each topic with H1 will not work, as there should only be one topic worthy of an H1 tag on a single page – if you believe that content deserves an H1 tag, create a new page for it. Equally, if there's only one major topic or 'point' to the page, add your H1 tag, but don't be tempted to add others for the sake of it.

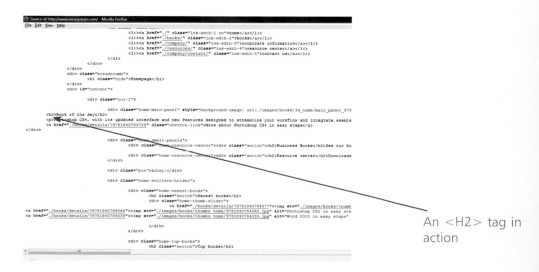

An <H2> tag in action

Search Engine Marketing

SEM, Paid Search or PPC Advertising to give this discipline just some of the many names it has, is a broad subject that will require some research on your part, before you should invest heavily.

SEM allows you to display an advert on the Search Engine Results Pages or on the Search Engine's network of publisher websites which you can target to display only to users searching for specific keywords or phrases related to your business. You control your account through an extensive back office, from the text or images of the advert to how much you wish to spend per day.

If you elect to run PPC ads with Google, then your ads will be displayed above and to the right of the organic or natural search results, i.e. the sponsored area. Google calls its program AdWords and it is how the Search Engine makes the vast majority of its money. Search Engine Marketing is effective because:

● It's quick to get started

● You can control your budget

● Your business is on an equal footing with other advertisers

● Your campaigns give you instant visibility even if you're not yet performing well on natural search

Beware

Test your adwords campaigns with a small budget to learn how it works.

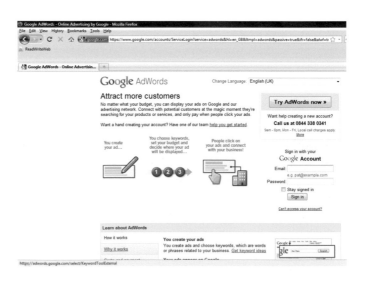

What Google has done with AdWords is essentially create an online auction for every keyword and phrase in every language. The more competitive a keyword, the more the price goes up... and this is how Google makes its money. Hundreds of thousands, if not millions of businesses around the world (big and small) all paying their pennies and dollars bidding on keywords.

Setting up an account is really simple, but do take the time to read the help and FAQs provided on the site – Google knows how its system works and have taken the time out to explain it all; it just requires you to sit down, uninterrupted, to read through the data and see how it applies to your website and your industry. AdWords does work, but depending on your industry the current price for some keywords (such as Business Consultant or Microsoft Software Training) may not necessarily be cheap.

Don't forget

There are a number of useful SEM resources listed in Chapter 8.

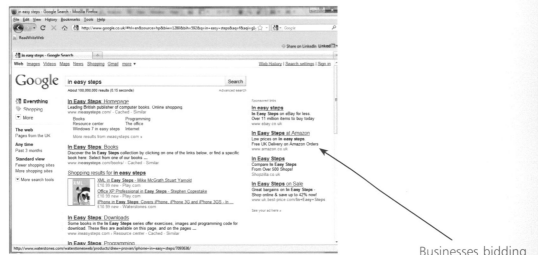

Businesses bidding on 'In Easy Steps'

AdWords works by charging you a fee (your bid price), every time someone clicks on your advert – the more you are willing to pay in comparison to others bidding for the same keywords and the better your landing page is (Quality Score) the higher up the sponsored links you will be placed. The bigger your daily budget, the more users will be shown your advert and the more that will (hopefully) click through. As soon as your budget has been spent, your advert is taken off until the next day. This allows you to keep tight control of your online marketing spend and allows you to see very quickly if the campaign is working (conversions) and to measure your return on investment.

Buying Traffic

Yep, it's true, you can buy pretty much anything on the internet, and that includes traffic to your website!

Buying traffic has a bit of a bad reputation, mainly because there are some unsavory businesses out there that will charge you for 10, 20, 500,000 visitors and not deliver, or just send a piece of software that replicates visits on your server logs, but is in fact a bot doing the job of people.

Just to be clear, when you pay to place a banner on another website, or when you pay for an Adwords campaign you are, in essence, trying to buy traffic. You want people who see your banner or advert to click through to your website.

Legitimate performance marketing companies do exist around the world and they are well aware of your need for traffic, but more importantly understand that you don't just want any old visitor, but traffic that is interested in your particular product or service range.

Enter performance marketing in the form of targeted email blasts and contextually-delivered landing pages.

Performance marketing companies invest heavily in building up their own network of users or publisher websites which they then exploit by showing their advertiser's (i.e. your) sales message to their network.

By carefully categorizing or segmenting their user base, they can confidently display your sport shoes landing page to users interested in sport shoes, or send an email with your advertising to users who have expressed an interest in sports shoes.

Depending on the size of the performance marketing company and the extent of their segmentation techniques you can specify the countries in which you want your advert to be shown or even the approximate age or gender of your target audience.

The more specific your requirements, the more you will be charged per sale or lead, but being performance-based, you only pay when the campaign results in a conversion, so it's win-win.

Hot tip

Know in advance how much a new customer acquisition costs your business.

- Burst! www.burstmedia.com

- DoubleClick www.doubleclick.com

- FastClick www.fastclick.com

- Aedgency www.aedgency.com

Be aware that some, but not all, performance marketing companies continue to utilize adware and/or pop up, or pop under web pages to display your advert. As browsers become more and more feature-rich the days of pop ups are indeed limited, but this channel is an option, and without doubt a strong landing page displayed to the right target audience will result in conversions at a very reasonable price.

Email Marketing

Email marketing through performance marketing companies, is an effective way to send your message via email before you've had the opportunity to build up your own database of customers.

Often segmented by interest, rented lists can provide a healthy return on investment.

Check with the provider that their lists are fully opt-in – i.e. each and every email address owner on their lists has expressly given their consent to receive 3rd party promotional emails

A recommended company operating in this sphere in both the UK and USA is Intela:

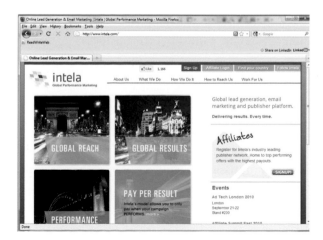

Affiliation (As Advertiser)

There are numerous affiliation networks available, most are generic, marrying a wide range of advertisers to publishers, however there are some industry or channel specific networks that have chosen to concentrate on one single market, e.g. casinos or health products.

How Does It Work?

Most networks charge new advertisers a set up fee which gives your business access to the network of affiliates and to the portal which allows you to choose and approve your affiliates. Be warned, affiliation is big business and set up fees can be anywhere from $1000 to $5000. In addition, most networks charge advertisers a monthly 'management fee' which covers your continued access to the network, a dedicated account manager, tips, tricks and advice about making affiliation work for your business.

Through the network's portal you will be able to set your payout percentages, monitor how many leads or sales have been generated and run reports to assess your affiliates' performance.

Paying on performance

The strongest aspect of affiliation is payment on performance. You only pay a commission if your affiliate delivers a lead, a registration or a sale.

You are free to pay as much or as little as you want for each of these conversions, but you will be matched against competitors so offering way less will not endear you to affiliates and they will be unlikely to want to pick up your campaign. Likewise, paying out too much may get you noticed by affiliates, but they are generally wise to the market and the product they promote and will be suspicious if you are paying out considerably more than the rest of the industry – it won't make you look generous, it will cause suspicion about the quality of your product and service.

Don't forget

If you're serious about generating volume, affiliation is a must.

A successful technique is to offer different payout tiers based on volume. For example 6% on 1-49 sales, 8% on 50-99 sales etc. This reward structure encourages affiliates to really get behind your campaign and strive to deliver the volume you require. Many advertisers also offer monthly or quarterly prizes to over-achieving affiliates – this is a sure way to pique interest in your campaign and keep affiliates on side.

Affiliates take campaigns very seriously and invest a lot of time, money and effort to promote advertiser's products and services.

Treat your affiliates well, as you would your own internal sales force. Keep them up to date with new products, new pricing and of course any offers or promotions you are planning to run. Good affiliate relations are all about good communication and when you find a hardcore of publishers who enjoy promoting your business, it can alter the fortunes of your business considerably.

Vouchers/Coupons

Vouchers and coupons are one of the strongest offline marketing techniques that have been successfully transferred online.

Coupons also offer your business the opportunity to attract offline customers to your online presence, or vice versa which makes the deployment of coupons something every online business should consider.

Hot tip

Customers love coupons! They're easy to distribute and they work.

Will using coupons devalue your brand? Business owners and marketing managers often worry that offering coupons may create negative connotations with their existing or target customer base – that in someway coupons cheapen an image or take away from the exclusivity of a brand, or educate users to expect a discount with every single purchase…

There are arguments for and against, but with the growth of mobile or m-commerce the explosion of social media platforms such as Facebook and Twitter, the distribution and user-acceptance of coupons has never been higher.

The pre-internet demographic of the 'average coupon user' changed radically when we all went digital – well-heeled, well-educated professionals have no qualms entering a 5 digit code on a website or scanning their iPhone at a sales counter to enjoy 10% off…

...cont'd

As a tool to create brand awareness, new customer acquisition and repeat purchases, you'd be very blinkered indeed to blow the idea out of the water, without giving it some serious consideration and even a controlled low-key test. If your offer's strong enough and open to new users, there's no reason why your own customer base won't assist in the distribution of a coupon by forwarding it to all their friends… go viral, go coupon!

To offer coupons on your site will require some back-end and front-end development work, so this needs to be specified and budgeted. If you're using a website platform such as Magento, the feature can be added for next to nothing.

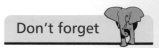

Don't forget

You can limit coupons to existing customers only, if you want to limit their availability.

Benefits:

- Relatively cheap to implement

- Everyone loves an offer

- Making the terms of the offer date specific encourages a quick ROI

- Easy to distribute

- Can be used to reward/encourage customer loyalty

- Add to your email marketing campaigns to help increase performance

Making Coupons Work

Coupons usually allow a new or an existing customer to benefit by entering a code at the point of purchase. The utilization of this code will modify the customer's order in some way usually changing one of the following: the price to be paid for the product/service or delivery, upgrading the shipping option, adding a free or discounted additional product, or adding value to the order such as free gift-wrapping.

Beware

Use codes rather than real words such as 'Free' or customers will create their own coupons.

These coupons can be printed and distributed through print media, handed out in the street as flyers or as part of your promotional literature, quoted on radio adverts or added to press releases etc. Or, they can be distributed online by adding the coupon code to a social media post such as your Twitter account or Facebook Fan Page, sent to existing customers in an email marketing blast or even added to the site such as in the following example:

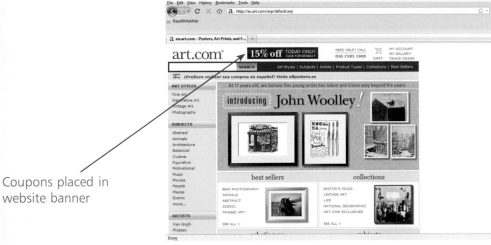

Coupons placed in website banner

You can test different coupons, of differing values, at different times of the year to better understand how your existing and new customers react.

Coupons work for service providers too – i.e. offering a discount off the next consultancy or service order, adding extra benefits or add-ons to a package – i.e. book now and pay for 12 language lessons and get an extra 3 lessons free with this coupon...

Cashback

Cashback is a relatively new but exciting development in the world of affiliation. Traditionally affiliates earn a commission every time one of their users performs an action leading to a sale or a lead for the advertiser.

The difficulty for affiliates was securing a second (or third) sale. Once the customer is aware of and has bought from the advertiser site, there is little need for the affiliate middle-man. Therefore, an affiliate earned only one commission from each user. Cashback was the solution that changed this model. Websites such as www.quidco.co.uk, www.deenero.es and www.bing.com/cashback/ are, in essence, super-affiliate websites. They offer links to advertiser websites or products or services and earn a commission in the usual way, but to ensure that customers come back to them in the future, and don't just go direct to the advertiser, the affiliate shares the commission they earn with the customer! That's right, customers who buy a new pair of shoes via a cashback website 'earn' or receive a percentage of what they spend given back to them in the form of cash. Not bad.

There are mixed feelings in the internet industry about cashback or incentivized traffic, some advertisers believe in the model, and others refuse to take part; worried it devalues their brand and leads to expectation from consumers never to pay full-price…

If you are considering affiliation in general, then consider cashback too – the amount of commission you pay out remains the same, it's just that the affiliate (in this case the cashback website) is choosing to share their commission with a third-party (i.e. your customer).

Co-Registration

Co-Registration is a lead and customer acquisition strategy used by a wide range of brands. Performance-based, i.e. you only pay on results, Co-Registration involves placing a short text or image advertisement for your company on the registration pages of high volume third-party websites or landing pages.

Usually, you are sharing the page with other advertisers who sell similar products or services, or, the page is themed in such a way as to link the advertisers – e.g. sign up with company x and get a discount when you buy from company y.

This method of promotion allows users to request additional information about your product or service and in turn provides you with their all-important contact details. As the customer has opted in, you are then at liberty to send promotional information about your products or service.

Co-Registration allows you to build a permission based, targeted database of consumers interested in your products, services, company, brand or special offers. And, depending on the volume of the third-party site, large lists can be accumulated very quickly.

The information captured by the Co-Registration service typically consists of a name, email address, IP address, registering URL and, in some cases, even a telephone number – this all depends on the Co-Registration form, but you will certainly have enough information with which to segment and contact these new leads.

Co-Registration aficionados claim it's increasingly complex to acquire new clients through traditional lead generation methods (pay-per-click, SEO, email marketing) so marrying with other brands for the purpose of a promotion (in which one or all of you are piggybacking off each other's brand) makes marketing much easier. The problem for website marketers is not in the acquiring of new prospects through Co-Registration but ensuring that the leads from a Co-Registration network are genuine and, of course, actually convert to buyers.

Beware

Do your research on the Co-Registration provider before committing.

Co-Registration Critical Points

● Click-through rates may be lower than you experience for in-house lists

● Customers who register through Co-Registration do tend to unsubscribe sooner; but remember they are less 'engaged' with your brand

● Make sure the prize or offer being advertised on the Co-Registration form is relevant to your product or service. A chance to win an iPod is all very well, but it has nothing to do with your accountancy business

● Make your offer attractive – customers must feel like they're getting a good deal which makes signing up right now necessary

● Before you sign a contract for any Co-Registration deal, ask for detailed audience demographics and check the traffic and popularity of those sites at Web properties such as Ranking.com or Alexa.com

● Only capture the essential data that you need to make the lead useful, e.g. a short form that asks for name and email is easier for your Co-Registration provider to incorporate. An offer that requires detailed information from the user (IP addresses, gender, age, location, etc.) necessitates greater customization and therefore dramatically raises your cost per lead

● Agree in advance with the provider what is to be done with duplicate or bad data – you should not have to pay for repeat entries from the same lead, nor for dummy or software-generated leads. It is quite common for as much as 10% of the leads generated to be rejected

● Use auto-responders to acknowledge receipt of the registration and to drive leads to act on your unique selling proposition

Don't forget

Co-Registration can result in a massive increase of potential customers.

137

Rich Media

Adding rich media such as videos, pod-casts, games etc. is a sure way to differentiate yourself from the competition, get noticed by other websites and invariably improve your visibility, content and reputation which in turn leads to a better natural Search performance.

Rich media was once the exclusive bastion of huge multi-national websites with marketing budgets to burn. Not now. With the ever-decreasing price of technology, an abundance of online or offline software tools, adding quality video to your site is well within everyone's reach.

"I'm an accountant, what on earth do I want to add video to my site for?" – You don't have to be a trained actor, you just need a script and the courage to press record...

Customer's love the personal touch and when you're providing a service, they want to know you know what you're talking about and a short (30-60 seconds is fine) video does just that.

By introducing yourself, your company and your services, customers can get an understanding of how you work and what you do, without having to read pages and pages of text. If you're completely camera shy, then of course you can hire professionals to act and record your message.

If you're selling products, a short video giving customers value added information, such as product tests, interviews with the manufacturer, how it was made, the product in real life situations, all make your website the one to visit.

Adding humor, true value-added advice or opinion will make your video watchable and attractive to users. When users like something they link to it, bookmark it, comment on it and generally help you to promote your business.

At the top end of the scale is the online game. Adding a game to your site can also create a buzz, links, traffic and exposure. If the game is good, it will be distributed by others increasing its reach and your returns.

Hot tip

Rich media is cheap to produce.

RSS Feeds

Really Simple Syndication is a service you can add to your website to engage with users. Your customer or visitor elects to receive your RSS feeds and by doing so is opting in to receive information from you, be it your latest blog post, site update notifications or specific messages you write for your RSS audience.

RSS is, by name and nature, simple – your chance to provide a text-based summary or teaser to an article, page or item of interest. If they're interested, they click through to read more. RSS works on so many levels because it is *simple*, the customer opts to receive it and you avoid having to create and pay for an email marketing campaign.

It's possible to create a buzz and encourage sign-ups by releasing exclusive content or offers to RSS subscribers only.

What Content Should You Include?

Anything and everything – if a customer has elected to receive RSS feeds from you, they are interested in your product, service or in you. By all means adopt a specific tone for RSS feeds but keep the feeds short, specific and tease the reader into clicking on the link to find out more – once your user has clicked, you have them back on your site which means you can wow them with your images, design and even more great content.

Don't forget

RSS is really simple to set up, plan to have feeds available from launch.

Social Media

Social media, why all the hype? Facebook is now the second highest trafficked site in the world* with more than 400 million users and growing.

Phrases like Web 2.0, the semantic web, social buzz, m-commerce and digital marketing may or may not mean something to you, but what they're all pointing to and what we're all heading towards is an online world where your website is no longer necessarily the conduit through which customers interact with your online business or your brand – your business has to be truly digital and that means having a presence on social media platforms that complements your website, extends the reach and appeal of your brand and engages users through the devices and applications with which they engage.

Hot tip

Social Media is the future of the web, get involved now, not later.

Beware

Effective social media management takes time and effort, dedicate resources to this.

Markets have in effect become fluid conversations and in order to be heard, to be seen and to be regarded as 'connected', your company has to participate in these real-time conversations. Having a social media presence is essential to actively manage the reputation of your brand.

*http://blog.performics.com/search/2010/03/free-and-paid-facebook-marketing-opportunities.html

By opening accounts with platforms such as Twitter, Facebook and Linked In you will be able to reach your potential audience and hear what is being said, create interest and buzz in your brand.

Listen, Be Accessible, Learn

Participating in conversations that involve your brand or industry will get you noticed and give you unparalleled insight into identifying your target clients and learning about your audience's needs – all in real time.

Participate, Engage, Relate

Simply setting up a fan page or an account is not enough, it's important to engage in one-to-one conversations which will leave a lasting impression and that turn potential users into real fans and actual consumers. Being seen to provide help, assistance and information resonates with your audience and quickly spreads via word-of-mouth – or more accurately, word-of-click.

Your users and clients want to be heard and will truly appreciate knowing somebody is behind your company ready to respond to their queries, generating added value. Embracing social media will help you succeed at being seen, being heard and satisfying your customers.

Blogging

You can look at blogging in two ways – like trying to keep a diary when you were young; in which you wrote furiously through most of January with the best of intentions but by February you were too busy and by March it was completely forgotten about. In simple terms, an annoyance. Or, you can treat blogging as a powerful marketing tool that helps build your brand, your customer base, links to your site and unique content which can only help your website perform better in natural Search.

Adding a blog to your business website is a simple procedure for any web developer and the quality and customization options from the big players such as Wordpress and Blogger leaves very little need to develop your own blog platform.

When writing articles for your blog it is essential to find an original angle and present news, comment and analysis in a fresh and engaging way. Try to inform customers rather than overtly trying to sell to customers. Well written blogs enjoy large readerships and if the content is of value, will be linked to, recommended, bookmarked and commented upon by not just potential customers, but by your competitors, industry experts and other interested parties.

Hot tip

Always write your blog offline, edit and then post online.

Beware

Take inspiration from other blogs, but don't cut and paste – write unique content.

Blogging helps:

- Brand building – your blog can become a destination for industry professionals and journalists as well as customers who want to know the latest information. Writing in a certain style can attract readers, but writing with authority is key

- New Customer Acquisition – a well-written blog that's quoted on other sites, linked to, referred or recommended will attract eyeballs and inevitably new customers for your product or service

- Customer Retention – Offering an RSS feed allows existing customers to stay abreast of your views and news, keeping your business in their radar and the value-added nature of a blog instills goodwill

- Reputation/Search Results – as you discovered in the SEO section earlier, performing well on natural Search relies heavily on your website's content, visibility and reputation. Regular blogging answers all three – your website will gain unique content, which in turn results in more inbound links which in turn leads to improved reputation

- If you take the step to include a blog on your website remember to update regularly. By default your blog posts are date stamped; a gap of a few weeks or even months looks bad. If you set yourself a specific blog day, stick to it

- Don't oversell through your blog – this isn't the media to push products or service, treat it as a way to pass comment or observations. By all means include links to products or services, but use an original angle in the blog and try to inform customers rather than overtly trying to sell to customers

- Competitive Advantage – if you're consistently the first blog or site to report on industry trends, new products or services, then you will be regarded as an authority – and therefore the first port of call for journalists looking to write a story

Don't forget

Blogging takes time, dedicate sufficient resources to do it properly.

Forums

Someone somewhere is talking about what you sell. Chances are, there are communities of like-minded people all furiously typing out their views and opinions, asking questions, seeking clarifications and generally getting involved. Why aren't you?

Hot tip

No matter how specific your industry, create a forum or group and see who you attract.

Beware

Forum or group membership tends to be short-lived, users come and go.

Adding a forum to your own site can be an effective way to capture the traffic interested in your product or service. Bolt-on open source solutions such as PHPBB are very easy to install and configure.

If you operate a forum on your website expect good and bad comments and allow your own time or someone else's to moderate the boards. It is essential to encourage differing opinions but obviously control malicious, damaging or offensive content.

Groups

A quick search on Google, or in Yahoo! Groups, Linked In, Xing etc. will give you an idea of both the quantity and size of existing groups that relate in some way to your business. Groups can be very local or totally international in scope. If you find that one doesn't exist, it's a 1 minute exercise to create your own group.

Don't forget

Add your URL to your signature block so that each message you post contains an identifier.

145

As with blogs, this isn't a suitable media to 'sell' your business; you will receive a backlash from other users and probably be banned from the discussion. You must offer other group members advice, help, and information.

Of course you can include a link to your website in your profile (as standard on most discussion forums). This is subtle marketing, in which you and your business are introduced to potential customers through your interaction, your ability to solve problems and your willingness to help.

Belonging to industry-related Groups is a really easy way to stay in the loop about what's going on in your field, but it's also a great idea to join Groups relating to topics in which you are less familiar. Surrounded by experts who are all willing to give out their advice and wisdom for free means you'll be up to speed in no time at all.

Targeting Print Media

Every single month new magazines launch and each of these publications is desperate for new original copy that will help sell copies and keep readers reading.

You may browse the magazine stands and think, yes, but they're all 'lifestyle' magazines, they don't relate to my industry or product… think again. It's all about the angle. Don't expect journalists to convert your robotic press release into an interesting feature – do it yourself!

- Create an angle by thinking outside the box – maybe an interesting way your product has been used by a consumer or company. Maybe your product or service usually appeals to one gender or consumer type… find someone who has broken the mold

- Magazines and newspapers are a mixture of text and image – include pictures with your press pack. If the story's of interest they may send their photographer to re-shoot, but your original image will pique their interest

- Write to the commissioning editor or journalist by name – it shows you've made an effort

- Keep trying – even if you've been rejected, submit a new press release at least every 3 months or when you genuinely have a newsworthy article – staff churn rate at magazines is high, and their focus can alter drastically, depending on circulation figures

- Consider an on-the-page offer. A competition prize is attractive as it's adding value to the magazine or newspaper – this could be a prize draw for registering or an online voucher code, discount or free information – be sure to create a specific unique webpage as the landing page so that you can track interest

Beware

Don't let your own prejudices influence your potential options – send your story to everyone.

Flyers

Your business may be online, but we all live in the physical world and old school marketing techniques such as flyers can be very effective.

Flyers are easy to produce and relatively cheap – the difficulty is distribution. Depending on your business and target market consider:

- Theatres, cafes, youth centers, cinemas

- Selective door-to-door postal drop

- Insert in local newspaper, national newspaper/magazine

- High street distribution

Flyers don't work all the time, it really depends on your product, service and target market. It is certainly worth printing a small batch which can be included in any physical mail you send, or used at any networking or speaking event.

Use the two sides effectively! Although one side will be your main message such as your range of products, or a specific promotion, the rear should have your pertinent contact details including web address, phone number and email address. If you have a physical office or storeroom and you're happy to receive clients, include that along with a simple map.

Freebies & Promotion

You might be running an online business, but you live in an offline world, and so do your customers. There are a number of ways to create exposure for your web address including:

Car livery/Graphics

Consider branding your own, your staff member's or your company cars with window stickers or a full *pimp-my-business* paint job. Assuming your website address is short and easy to remember, although your exposure is limited to when and where you drive, your web address will get around...

Corporate Giveaways

Mouse mats, pens, corporate gifts etc. – both the curse and the benefit of attending trade shows and exhibitions. Without doubt, branded freebies work. People do take them home and tend to use them.

Send out to repeat or valued customers as well as other companies in your industry – the items don't have to be serious, there have been incredibly successful branding campaigns involving yo-yos, hats, rear-view mirror trinkets etc.

Business Cards

You run and operate an online business, be sure your website address is clearly visible on your business card!

Radio & TV

Radio and television, as with print media offer you two routes. The expensive advertising route, and the less straight-forward but ultimately more valuable free feature or editorial coverage route.

Paid-for advertising, certainly on local radio, can be measured and for certain services and products is an effective way to attract local customer base to your offering and create brand awareness.

When deciding to advertise on the radio or via television, it's essential to research the viewer/listener profiles and figures and weigh up how suited they are to your brand. As a guess, your accountancy services are of little interest to the teenage listeners of CrazyHipHop.FM or similar.

Don't forget

Radio stations are desperate for content; write to a producer, you might be surprised.

As with print media, to get radio producers and television producers interested in your business, you have to angle the initial approach to show how your product or service range can benefit their audience and not try to overtly sell.

The key to this is to look for the lifestyle angle. If, for example, you're female, have an ethnic minority heritage, a non-heterosexual lifestyle, successfully triumphed over, or find yourself coping with, illness, disability or bereavement; or, if you are under 30 or over 60, these are all angles from which you can make your initial approach to commissioning editors/producers. Of course you have to be 100% comfortable with marketing yourself and your business in this way, but without doubt, it opens doors, and gets you airtime and column inches which you can use to heavily promote your business.

Press Releases

Every online business is competing for press coverage. There are only so many physical inches of newspapers published every day and only so many online authority news or industry-related websites; therefore it's essential that your press release gets to the right editor, is noticed, and the content gets transformed into a feature or article.

Good PR is all about putting yourself in the position of the journalist or editor. If you received over 100 press releases a week, but you only have seven articles to write, what's going to help you choose which stories to run?

Target Your Audience

You're wasting your time and the editor's time if your business or the angle is completely unrelated to the publication's usual fare. This may sound obvious, but new businesses sometimes try the scatter gun approach in the hope that something, anything, sticks. Your 'new maternity wear range' press release is more likely to be picked up by a lifestyle/female orientated/baby-related publisher than a financial services publisher...

Having said that, if you can angle your article to show how your maternity wear is ideal for the workplace with a few images of suitably dressed power-mums-to-be sporting your latest range, you may be in luck!

Hot tip

Research your target magazines or papers, write to the same word length.

Do Your Research

Find out the name of the editor or writer and address the Press Release to them specifically. This is just a common courtesy and is the equivalent of someone phoning your business and asking to speak to the CEO, or asking to speak to you personally, by name.

Check And Double Check

Make sure any facts are indeed correct, especially when it comes to numbers, as these are the easiest element that can be checked by a researcher or journalist. Always show generic industry figures to help put your claims or story in some sort of context.

Spelling & Grammar

Have someone else proofread your text; mistakes reflect badly on you and your business and it's another excuse for your release to be ignored. Keep sentences short and snappy and if necessary, include a glossary or definition of industry terms.

Timing

Consider publishing deadlines; magazines are written well in advance of their publication date, i.e. the June edition is usually in the shops in late May and being written in March and April at the very latest. So if you want a magazine to feature aspects from your '100 hot bikinis' release, you need to be talking to them in February.

Angle

So, you've added an additional luxury product range to your website, or you've branched into Conveyancing to complement your existing Family Law services... So what? Who cares? Why is that news, and why should an editor use their valuable space to promote you? You need to give the publication an angle, something unique, quirky or interesting that can make your press release relevant, interesting and exciting for their audience... For local newspapers or radio make sure there is a human hook.

Marketplaces

Marketplaces such as eBay which is now enjoying its second decade of success, is, quite frankly a genius invention that has revolutionized how we buy and sell. Although eBay was conceived with the idea to enable individuals to buy and sell among themselves, it wasn't long before a facility for professional sellers was added.

eBay and Amazon in the USA and UK and Priceminister and Play in Europe among others provide online businesses with the opportunity to enjoy a worldwide audience by listing your products or services and offering them to their enormous customer bases.

Hot tip

If you have a large product database, look at investing in an API or XML export.

Beware

Marketplace customers tend to be much more price sensitive.

By paying a listing fee, and/or a monthly subscription plus a percentage or share of the sale price, your business gains unprecedented reach in a matter of days.

Professional Sellers

To make it easy for businesses to sell via marketplace sites, eBay etc. offer a route to professional sellers to be able to bulk load their products. This is done via XML, CSV or through an online portal. There is some work involved on your side adapting your product database to the platform's particular product classification rules, but once that's done, it's usually a straightforward process loading hundreds or even hundreds of thousands of products.

The listing fee, commission on sale and any monthly membership fees can be a little high if you are selling low-margin products such as music, consumer electronics or books, but the sheer size of audience that these marketplace platforms offer makes it worthwhile.

Other than time, initial investment to be up and running on these platforms is very low and therefore it is well worth exploring as a viable channel for your e-commerce business.

Chapter Summary

- Online and Offline marketing will help promote your business and grow awareness, generally online marketing is the cheapest and most cost-effective

- SEO is your best friend – learn about the subject, become passionate about it and be sure you or someone in your business is looking after the strategy. Done right it is the single most effective way to grow your business

- Don't obsess over a handful of keywords – explore the long tail and optimize your site for a rich variety of phrases that are actually being used by your potential customers

- Paid Search is a powerful tool in your armoury, but research it well before investing money

- The traffic you need for your website is out there – the best way to help that traffic find your website is by being everywhere they are. Invest in affiliate and performance marketing. Spread your net wide and you will net growth

- If you're running an e-commerce store, customers love coupons and cashback – you will take a small hit on every sale, but build large followings of dedicated customers who will in turn tell their friends…

- If you're not a writer, find someone on your team who is – the need for great content affects your entire marketing mix, from SEO and SEM, to press releases, blogs, social media and good old-fashioned email… content is king

- Let your customers connect to you through forums, social media, questionnaires, email and even via telephone – listen to what they say, engage, empathize and show the world you care and respond – this will build your reputation above your competitors

7 Customer Relationship Management

It's fair to say that if you throw enough money into marketing, you will find customers. But the most successful online businesses are those that know how to retain those customers and have them coming back for more… In this Chapter we will explore Customer Relationship Management.

Delivering Good CRM

Customer Relationship Management should be the cornerstone of your business. Without customers you have no business; so looking after them, their experience, their needs and their wishes before, during and after they buy a product or service from you, is paramount to running a successful online business.

Managing expectations is all about living up to your promises. Do what you say you're going to do and customers will be happy.

- If you say you ship products within 24 hours, make sure it ships, or inform the customer about the delay

- If you advertise a customer service phone number, have staff answering calls during the advertised hours

- If the item comes with a free gift, or an upgrade – be sure to include it

- If you offer the 'cheapest' prices on the web, check they remain the cheapest; and offer the customer a refund of the difference if they find a cheaper offer elsewhere

- If you promise to call back customers, be sure that you do

This may all seem like common sense, but so many companies fail on the small stuff, and take their customer base for granted. Disgruntled customers talk with their feet, or more accurately in the online arena, take their e-wallet directly to your competitor.

It's essential that your online business promotes something that customers want, or need. Without a basic desire for your products or your services, it's going to be hard to find customers and harder still to sell to them, but when you acquire a customer it's imperative for your reputation, future sales and your bottom line that you treat each customer with respect and due care and attention.

If there's only one rule to take from this book, then it is 'treat your customers as you would wish to be treated yourself'. Maybe it is a cliche but it's true!

Accessibility

With the rise and rise of mobile devices, never before has accessibility been such a hot topic. Ensuring that mobile or tablet-based users can access a website and its features will be the next battle-ground for web designers and developers as well as online businesses and should certainly be on your priority list, if it isn't already.

But accessibility goes a lot further than just new ways to access the web. Accessibility means providing the means for disabled, blind, deaf or senior web users to engage with your website and its content.

Accessibility, more so than ever before, is also one of the ways to get into bed with Google. Google, unlike human users, can't read the beautiful images on your site, Google only sees the filenames of the images, not what may be written in the image on the website. Therefore, Google likes and rewards websites that are W3C compliant – this means clean code, clear navigation and a text-based alternative if your website employs rich features such as JavaScript, AJAX or Flash. To find out if your website is W3C compliant visit the W3C site and input your URL to their free validator tool. The good news is that the response highlights precisely the line or lines of code that will need to be altered (and what needs to be altered):

Don't forget

With the explosion of mobile devices, accessibility has never been more important.

Respectability

To win the hearts and minds of a customer is a long process which begins the moment they see an advert, banner, link, business card or any mention of your website address.

The customer's journey and relationship with you begins on that first click and you've got to impress from then on. Is your homepage or landing page delivering on what the advert or link promised? How straightforward is it for customers to order the product they want from you, or to contact you about your services?

Gaining Respectability

The fly-by-night nature of the web is both an advantage and a disadvantage when you're launching your own online business. On the positive side, as you've learnt, you can quickly create a web presence which gives the impression of a large established organization; done right, customers will flock to your virtual doors. On the flip side, because it is so easy to create a website and there exists a plethora of beautifully created but essentially fraudulent websites out there, canny customers will always proceed with caution.

Gaining respectability starts with your homepage, and how well that is received, but your entire website and proposition must stand up to the same scrutiny, not to mention the order pipeline, your email/phone interaction with the customer and of course your delivery – be it a product or a service. Then there's your after-sales care or follow up and your email marketing campaigns, PR and what folks are saying about you through social media sites… Respectability on the web is hard won and fast lost.

Beware

Building respectability takes time, it's not an overnight operation.

Contact Details

Both a legal requirement and a courtesy – you must include a contact phone number on your website, to allow customers to contact you.

Although the primary objective of your website may be to sell products or services online – this is not necessarily why somebody has come to your website.

It is imperative that you offer users the chance to find out the information they want. This is usually achieved through a help page, a search box or a FAQ page but you simply can't second-guess every user about what they might be looking to find on your site; a phone number gives them another option, and, even if they don't use it, seeing it there instills confidence in your brand and service – you're clearly not hiding.

Crucially, if you're selling products online, add the phone number to the pages of the order pipeline. A percentage of customers abandon the order process having successfully placed an item in their basket – by offering a phone number, if they're experiencing difficulties, or become confused, that phone number offers the chance for you to catch the sale (and possibly up sell!). Don't expect users to navigate to your Contact Us page to find the information – add it to the page!

Phone number on every page

Legal Pages

Terms And Conditions

We're all guilty of accepting terms and conditions without reading a single word of them. This habit is unlikely to change and it is shared across the world. For you as a user this isn't too much of a problem, but for you as a business owner the terms and conditions of your website is a critical topic.

Having customers visiting your website is no different to having customers visiting your physical offices or high street store. Your website is your online presence through which your brand is represented and information is being presented.

It is therefore essential that your website terms and conditions outline exactly what is expected of users using your website, and what your users can expect from you. Seek professional legal assistance with the creation of this very important document.

Privacy Policy

A privacy policy, generally, is a single page document stating your company policy regarding what customer information you collect, and what you plan to do with it, now and in the future.

The rise and rise of online identity theft has made customers suspicious, especially of websites with which they are unfamiliar.

When constructing your privacy policy, think long and hard about what you plan to do with customer information, and with that in mind, create a document which covers the following aspects:

- What information do you collect from users of your website?

- What information do you store?

- What do you do with that information?

- Why do you collect that information?

- What do you plan to do with it in the future?

- What will happen to that data should the ownership of your business change?

Hot tip

Don't cut and paste legal documents from another website, write your own.

Beware

Should you alter your privacy policy in the future, alert customers via a newsletter.

Invoice/Receipt

When providing a service or selling a product to a customer, it is your legal responsibility to provide an invoice/receipt with the purchase which should contain the following information:

- Invoice Number – a unique identifying number specific to that customer's order. (Don't use sequential numbering as it is easy for competitors to track how many orders you ship)

- Invoice Date – the date the order was placed by the customer – for online orders this is the date the customer confirmed their order and provided payment details

- VAT number – if you are VAT registered, this number must be displayed. If your client is VAT registered, you must also include their VAT number

- Registered Address – the registered address of your company (this can be different to your trading address). If it is different, be sure to highlight the address you want customers to use for queries and returns

- Company Registration Number – as a registered company, you must include your registration number and the country or state where you are registered

- Product/Service Details – name and identifying number of product/s or service

- Quantity – confirm how many items a customer ordered and it assists with stock management, shipping and customer services

- Price paid – the exact amount the customer was billed for the order. Separate the product prices from postage and packing as, depending on your location and the location of your customer different rates of tax may apply

- Payment method – how was the order paid for? Specify card type and last four digits, or check, or bank transfer

- Tax paid – highlight the amount and rate of sales tax or VAT that is being applied to the order

- Customer's full name and address – who, or which entity, is being invoiced?

Tone Of Voice

Decide upon a distinct tone for all your communications and stick to it – it doesn't have to be formal, just consistent and in keeping with your brand and your target audience. Having a unique tone can be the key to winning customer trust, winning valuable press coverage and ensuring that it's your brand and your website that users click on and recommend to others.

It's obviously possible to alter your company tone of voice over time, but deciding on what you want from the start will be far more effective. For an example of a distinct tone which has won a company customers and reputation check out Innocent:

Hot tip

If all of your competitors use serious tones on their site – consider being more zany!

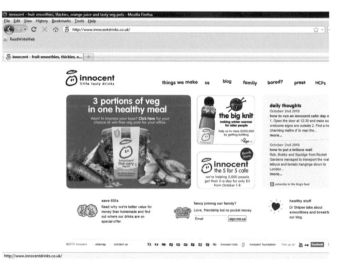

Beware

Have fun with your tone, but you must convey your message to customers.

Creating a unique, witty or off-the-wall style will immediately get you noticed and help differentiate your site from the raft of competitors out there. Certain topics or professions may limit your ability to get creative – after all you're unlikely to drum up much divorce advice business for your law firm if you make light of the client's situation or circumstances – however, including a well thought out diagram of the divorce process and a bullet-pointed list explaining how your firm can help, will sell your services far better than pages and pages of legalese that confuse your reader.

Be different, inform, engage.

Going Above & Beyond

You're a new business and you have to impress potential and returning customers – giving away something for free may seem counter-productive but it can be super effective at ensuring future custom and causing a word-of-mouth stir. This is true for both product and service providers.

For Product Providers:

- Give away something novel i.e. a free packet of sweets/candy bar with every order

- Upgrade random customers' delivery options – under promise over deliver

- Include a voucher or code for a discount of future purchases

- Offer a reward for introducing a friend to your service

For Service Providers:

- A PDF guide or white paper on a topic of interest to potential clients available for download – if it's branded, you'll get the call… i.e. see http://www.aedgency.com/resources/guides/

- An invitation to some of your best clients to join you on a night out

- Offer a reward for introducing another company to your service

- Run a fantasy football or similar league for your clients with an attractive prize for the winner

- Create an award – e.g. if you are an accountant launch a competition via your website or create a micro-site for the best business plan – you'll have a great chance to get media coverage, traffic and all those new businesses will need accounting services…

You can use one or all of these techniques at different times of the year – your aim always is to delight your customers.

Customer Services

Customer services does not just mean offering a phone number or an email address on the site and hoping for the best.

To manage your expectations, if you're operating an e-commerce operation, you'll be very lucky indeed if your customer contact rate is less than 5-10%. This means for every 100 orders you ship, at least 5-10 people will contact you before, during or after their order. Of those same contacts about 50% will contact you again with a follow up inquiry. You must allow for this in your daily operations and have suitable staff allocation in place.

At first you will be able to handle the calls and the emails yourself, but for all the time you are answering a customer, or finding out what happened with their order, either internally or with the carrier, you're not doing the other twenty tasks that need to be done.

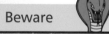

Beware

Skimping on customer service will cost you reputation.

For service providers, customer services also covers sales inquiries and client care, both pre- and post-sale. These inquiries won't be so numerous, but without doubt each inquiry will be unique and will require a detailed and well researched response. Again, you will be able to handle this yourself initially, but eventually it will require its own resource.

Your tone with customers (or potential customers) must at all times be professional and courteous – it could be that one initial email that leads to a huge order or turns out to be from a journalist writing a piece on your particular market.

...cont'd

It could be that this same customer becomes one of your most loyal and constant clients recommending you far and wide. Your customers are your lifeblood and customer service is therefore a very necessary arm of your business, not something you can try and 'deal with' whilst eating your lunch.

- Clearly display a phone number on your website, especially during the order pipeline pages

- Provide email addresses or contact forms for customers to contact you

- Consider live chat functionality for customers who require an immediate response

- Give customers a guide to when they can expect a reply – if it's 24 hours, make sure you reply within this time frame

- Fix the customer's problem as quickly and efficiently as you can

- Take any criticism seriously and investigate what you can do to stop the same thing happening to other customers

Without doubt many of your customer's inquiries will have similarities and therefore it's well worth creating templates or blurbs which can be utilized for the most common types of contact. Don't send the template out without editing, as no single email can cover so many bases.

- Personalize the email with the customer's name, order number/reference, delivery address

- If the contact is related to a credit or debit card number, be sure that neither you nor the customer quotes the card number via email – this must be done via an http webpage or via telephone/fax

- Quote the expected or revised delivery date if applicable

- Sign off with a real name, so that the customer can follow up with the customer service representative in the future

- Thank the customer for their query/order/comment

Don't forget

Engage with customers direct through tools like Twitter.

Newsletters

Newsletters are very specific mailings and should not be confused or grouped together with email marketing campaigns.

The easiest way to differentiate the two is to remember that a newsletter cannot include a sales-related call to action.

Here are some examples:

- Hired new staff – include a bio and contact details and outline the area/s of business the new staff member will be looking after

- New offices – great for kudos and essential to let clients know your new contact details

- Recruitment drive – let your client list know that you're hiring – you know they like your product and service; it shows that you're growing and it's a great way to 'sell' your business

- New white paper / free information available – you're giving it away for free, and it's of interest to your client base

The frequency of newsletters should be few and far between – we're all busy people and just because I've bought a book from you once or you fitted my new kitchen doesn't mean I want to get a weekly update of every single corporate decision you make forever. Remember – are your customers really interested in this? Will it help them?

Most importantly, customers must opt-in to receive newsletters. Ask the question when they register on your website and if they opt out, respect their decision.

As a rule of thumb, quarterly newsletters will be tolerated by most customers, and the frequency should only be broken if indeed there is time sensitive material that must be communicated to your user base, for example a major alteration to the ownership of the company, or changes to the privacy policy which affect how you treat customer data.

Hot tip

Once you've sent the newsletter, wait one week and then add the content to your website.

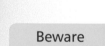

Beware

Some users will unsubscribe from your mailing list on receipt of a newsletter.

Questionnaires

Customers who use your website, who have bought a product or service from you in the past and who took the trouble to register with your website are a potential font of knowledge and advice, should you choose to listen to what they say.

When you're running your own website, it becomes increasingly difficult to be objective about the website and how your business operates – you're simply too deeply involved. Friends, family and staff may have opinions, but they tend to be favorable as no one wants to rock the boat.

Your customers, however, are brutally honest about what they like and what they don't like, and many will tell you, if you give them the opportunity. When creating a questionnaire think about the following:

- Be clear internally about what you are trying to achieve from the questionnaire

- Don't try to measure too much in a single questionnaire – it's better to focus on a single measurable aspect, such as web usability or product range, than try to ask customers about every aspect of your business

- Incentivise customers to complete the questionnaire – for example provide a coupon or enter the respondents into a competition to win a prize – customers value their time and helping you run your business isn't their priority

- Don't write leading questions, be as objective as possible

- Utilize scaled responses such as Very Satisfied, Quite Satisfied, Neither Satisfied nor Dissatisfied, Quite Dissatisfied, Very Dissatisfied

- Ensure customer privacy regarding responses

- Include the opportunity for customers to write comments or criticisms at the end of the questionnaire

- Use the data! There is absolutely no point running the operation if you don't react to what your customers tell you

Email Marketing

Email marketing, managed correctly, is one of the greatest customer retention tools in your arsenal. Managed incorrectly, your message will be ignored, your company email address filtered straight into the customer's Junk folder and very little chance indeed of any future custom or goodwill…

As well as being entrepreneurs, we are also consumers, and therefore you will be familiar with email marketing through your own inbox – promises of get rich quick schemes, Nigerian millions just waiting to be placed in your bank account, magic blue pills to turn you into Superman – even if you're female! This is spam, and its affect on all of us is to be suspicious of anything offered via email.

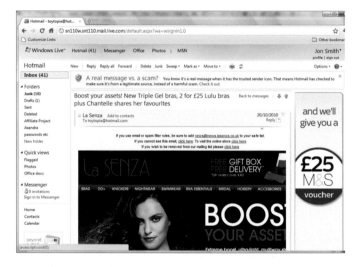

Opt In

The temptation is to add every email address you receive (from inquiries, from business cards, from customers who have placed an order or even from bought lists) and to add them to your mailing list. The rationale is that if they've shown an interest in your website then they'd love to hear about all your latest offers. Wrong. Not only is this ethically questionable, it's now illegal. Data Protection laws have finally caught up to the Internet and unless a customer has opted in specifically to receive your mailing list, you can't use their email address.

What if you take the risk anyway? You might get away with it, you might make a ton of sales. But if you get caught, you will be fined (we're talking significant six figure sums, depending on the territory) and all the hard work you've put into creating and running your online business is for nothing.

Opt In, means the customer has to physically check the box, to confirm they would like to receive email marketing. Semi-Opt-In (i.e. the checkbox is pre-checked) is the same as not asking for permission... don't do it.

Don't forget

There must be a hook to the email that will encourage users to click through to your site.

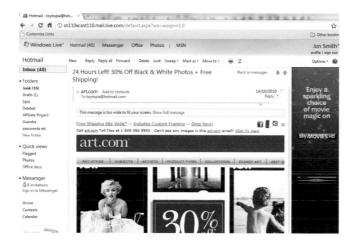

Frequency

There are no hard and fast rules about what is an acceptable frequency of emails. It is likely that you will try a few patterns to assess the effectiveness of campaigns. Some companies work on a monthly basis tying their messaging in with major holidays and festivals. Other companies mail their list at least once a week. You can't be all things to all people and that is why targeting is critical to the success of your online campaigns.

Selective Targeting

Whatever your product range or service offering, customers are not interested in everything you sell or do. Using the example of an accountancy website, your client first hired you to help with their company formation which you duly did – you know the client has a small manufacturing business. Sending that client email marketing about your new service for online retailers is a waste of your time and theirs...

Data Capture

Targeting can only happen if you have collected and correctly recorded/processed data. How and what to capture is a debate beyond the scope of this book and this very topic will have Customer Relationship Managers fighting to the death with Usability Managers. On one hand you want to capture as much as possible to accurately segment the database to improve targeting. On the flip side, if you ask too many questions, or you ask questions before you've built up trust and a relationship with a customer, they're not going to answer completely or accurately, which devalues the process and the data…

What's a girl to do? Well, at all times it's essential that you put yourself in the shoes of the customer and make decisions based on the customer journey through your site. When you're selling products online you want to make the process as straightforward as possible, and that means asking the minimum number of questions to allow quick progress through the order pipeline.

Effective data capture and targeting:

- On a customer's first visit or purchase ask as few questions as possible – you need to build trust first and show you can deliver on your core product or service

- After a customer's first purchase or after you have provided a service, follow up with a questionnaire asking the customer to rate aspects of the service. On this questionnaire you can add additional (optional) targeting questions – such as gender, age range, purchasing interests etc.

- People change email addresses – your database is full of defunct email addresses and continuing to send mails to these addresses is a waste of time and money. It will also negatively affect your statistics when you measure the effectiveness of campaigns. Cleanse your database of hard-bounces (emails that never arrived at the recipient's inbox)

- In the 'My Account' section on your website, empower users to alter their preferences and interest. By asking the customers which products or categories they are interested in, you will have the most accurate information available

Hot tip

A simple drop down that captures Mr, Mrs, Ms will allow segmentation by gender.

A/B Or Variate Testing

You will never be all things to all people and even if you employ the most accurate targeting imaginable, your email shoot will not convert every recipient all of the time. To improve your opening rate, click through rate and ultimately the conversion rate of campaigns, it's advisable to test different designs and copy and measure the results.

If you have identified 1000 registered users who have opted in to receive email marketing about one of your products or services, break this group into further smaller clusters – for example, four sets of 250. With each variant email, test a specific alteration such as the size and color of the action button, or the sales message in the opening paragraph, or the subject line…

It takes time, but over the course of a number of shoots, you begin to build a profile of what works for a specific group of your customers. There are learnings that can be applied across the board, and there will be interesting subtleties that seem unique to a particular sub-set of customers.

Record your findings and constantly optimize – remember that even a single percentage increase in your opening rate will impact the effectiveness of the entire campaign, and adding a single percentage increase to your conversion rate, can result in massive shifts in your profitability.

Don't forget

The smallest change to the design or copy can make a huge difference with conversion.

171

Email Tone & Content

You will have created and utilized a tone throughout your website copy and advertising creative. Your email marketing activities must also convey this tone to show the correlation between this campaign and your overall business. With email marketing there is the additional pressure of having to get an effective message across, quickly. Writing effective email marketing copy is a challenge. Here are the main pointers to remember:

1 The specific product, service or promotion

2 The benefit to the user

3 The action you require from the reader

The Specific Product, Service Or Promotion

It seems obvious but you must focus the mail on a specific product, service or promotion. A generic 'hey, we're here and we sell stuff' message is a waste of your time and your customer's. Decide on what you're going to promote and tailor the design, layout and text to support this choice.

The Benefit To The User

Just notifying the reader that you sell or provide something, is not enough. There needs to be a hook, to pique their interest and convince them they need your product or service. The benefit of course could simply be a very competitive price, if this is the case, ensure the imagery and copy highlight this fact. A benefit can be seasonal, related to a festival or on the service side; relating to changes in the market, law, technological improvements etc. The benefit to the user should also reinforce why the reader should choose you…

The Action You Require From The Reader

Make it easy for customers to do what you want them to do. If they need to click on a link or a button, make it obvious that it's a link or button and design the page so that everything (text, image, train of thought) leads to that one goal. If you require the reader to complete a form, keep the questions to a minimum and only capture what's absolutely essential for them to continue – by definition of the fact you have emailed the customer, asking for their name or email address are redundant steps.

Hot tip

Above all else, make the content of your emails 'interesting'.

Beware

Check, double check and triple check your email copy for errors before sending.

Managing Your Lists

As counter-productive as it may sound, you must offer your customers the option to Opt Out of future email marketing campaigns. Yes, they've said they want to receive emails, but this doesn't mean ad infinitum; it could be that a user was interested in receiving updates about offers for a particular period of time, or they were researching a particular product or service and now they are satisfied. Or, they're simply no longer interested in your business offering anymore…

Offering users the ability to Opt Out doesn't necessarily encourage users to abandon your service, it simply allows customers the chance to manage their affairs and thus instills goodwill and helps you manage your mailing list. Be sure to offer an Opt Out link at the bottom of every email marketing shoot, and within the My Account section of your website.

Cleansing Your Database

You're kidding yourself and negatively impacting your campaign statistics if you don't keep your email database clean and up to date. Continuing to send emails to addresses that no longer exist, no longer open your mails or no longer interact with your mails, is a waste of time and money. Purge your hard-bounces after every mailshot.

Re-activation mails should be sent to customers from whom you've received no interaction over the past six months – they haven't logged in to their account on your site, they haven't contacted you and they haven't clicked on an email marketing link.

A re-activation mail acknowledges that you haven't heard from/ seen a customer in a while, it reinforces your strengths and Unique Selling Points (USPs) and can even include a return incentive such as a discount code. Critically, you must offer the customer the opportunity to Opt Out and promise to remove the address from your list – if you win back the customer, great, but if they don't respond or Opt Out, you can be sure the customer is lost.

Yes, you'll have a leaner mailing list, but it will be an active database.

Mystery Shopper

Firstly, assuming you have at least one additional staff member or member of the management team, and even if you are launching a service-based website rather than selling products online, you can employ a mystery shopper.

What you are looking for is an impartial test of your entire proposition – from the accuracy of the content and statements you make about yourself and your product or service, to your actual ability to get the order right, deliver the correct product or service and to deal with any client question or dispute in a timely and mutually beneficial manner.

The devil is in the detail, and big or small your business must get the basics right. This means everything from answering email inquiries promptly, politely and providing the customer with the correct answer right through to ensuring your website is online, links point to where they should point and of course, you're able to provide the customer with what they want – be it a product or service.

● There is a cost to having a regular mystery shopper, and of course placing the occasional order or writing the occasional email won't catch every glitch, but it can expose simple failings that if they are happening to your mystery shopper, they are almost certainly happening to real customers...

- The mystery shopper can of course be you, but it's far better to arrange for a 3rd party to pose as a mystery shopper. This can be anything from a casual arrangement you have with a family member to a professional arrangement with a marketing firm. It's up to you

- Make sure the contact email address or delivery address (be it an inquiry, complaint or e-commerce order) is not easily recognizable (by you or any staff member)

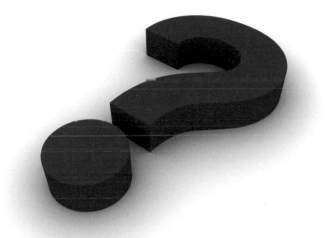

- Test your e-commerce delivery capabilities by placing orders at different times of the day, on different days and with an array of delivery addresses including international. Ensure the mystery shopper logs the time of order, and of course the date and time the order was received and in what condition

- Test your customer services through a range of simple and complex inquiries, order follow ups and complaints/concerns. How quickly were the emails answered and was the issue dealt with to the mystery shopper's satisfaction?

Focus Groups

A common misunderstanding about focus groups is that a single group during a single session can highlight all the problems with your website or service. The key word in all of this is 'focus' and the first rule is to ensure you are clear what exactly you want your group to focus on…

Groups you can run could include testing your website, but focus the group on a particular function – such as the internal search, browse, or the order pipeline.

Ensure The Group Is Well-Led

Preparation is everything. Ensure you have suitable space and equipment to run a focus group. Each participant is going to need access to a computer; they obviously have to be online if you're testing the live site, or networked with the correct permissions to access a development server or environment.

Have a staff member on hand to answer or assist participants, but this mustn't be hand-holding… if a user in the room doesn't know where to click, or how to find something on your website, you've got a problem that could be happening to real customers on a daily basis.

Record Everything

You want to be able to take away useful information from each and every participant. Prepare questions and/or tasks for your group. You may want them to order a specific product or browse for specific information. Track their behavior through your logs or employ eye-tracking or click-tracking software to understand how the participant interacts with your site.

Use Strangers

It's the easiest thing in the world to make a few phone calls and have a room full of friends, family members and acquaintances all eagerly smiling and happy to help you test your website...

If there's a connection, you're not going to get a completely honest response. Whether people subconsciously don't want to hurt your feelings, or due to recent conversations know what it is you're trying to achieve with the new site (or whatever you're testing) can sway or influence their opinion, and therefore your results. Find strangers!

Don't forget

Test small, test regularly.

Incentivize

We're all busy people and therefore need to be incentivized to take time out of our daily schedule to help you improve your business. How many times have you been surfing on a website only to see a pop-up window asking you to take part in a user survey?

Pay people a reasonable fee for their time – if the focus group is for more than a couple of hours, be sure to provide refreshments and of course offer access to a bathroom. It is only fair to cover transport costs and basically make it as easy and attractive as possible for people to come to help you.

Additional Feedback

There must be some time allocated to allow your participants to give feedback – be it through a written document or a Q&A session at the end. What are their feelings about the task/s, the website, the functions they were testing and how does it all compare to other websites they might use?

You might find that your participants are comparing your online clothes store to their favorite holiday booking site or their online banking experience, it doesn't matter... observe, learn, improve....

Chapter Summary

- Whatever claims or promises you make on your website, be sure you always deliver on them. Constantly check your internal processes and compare yourself to your competitors

- Ensure your site is accessible to mobile, disabled or older users as much as it is for able-bodied users – if it wasn't reason enough to be as inclusive as possible with your website, the knock-on benefits are an increased customer base as more and more users choose to surf the web via mobile devices, and Google will be able to access, index and rank your website

- Build respectability by giving customers constant visual clues to your business acumen – display your contact number/s and addresses clearly along with your terms and conditions and privacy policy

- If you're selling products or services, each and every customer must receive an invoice/receipt with every purchase

- Differentiate yourself from the competition by creating a unique tone, be it through text or imagery. Be better by being different!

- Go above and beyond customer expectations. Under promise and over deliver

- Customer Services is critical to your success – be accessible, be fair and listen to your customers

- Email is a powerful communication tool – use it for marketing and for newsletters, but clearly define your messages and ensure everyone on your email database list has opted in

- Test everything – the smallest of alterations can increase conversion rates by single or multiple percentage points. Never rest, even if you've got a webpage or email template that works well, run a 'b' version to improve it

- Have fun with your new business, listen to your customers, be successful

8 Useful Resources

Websites and specialist books are a fantastic source of further information regarding every topic covered in this book. This chapter lists some essentials.

Useful Resources

Starting your own online business is a big step and a big commitment. Depending on your background and experience, there may be areas in which you feel less equipped. Here are some resources to help you with your new venture:

Business Planning

The Definitive Business Plan – Richard Stutely

Business Plans: www.bplans.co.uk

Business Networks & Advice

Business Link: www.businesslink.gov.uk

Chamber of Commerce: www.britishchambers.org.uk

Federation of Small Businesses: www.fsb.org.uk

Business Gateway: www.bgateway.com

StartUps.co.uk: www.startups.co.uk

Linked In: www.linkedin.com

Xing: www.xing.com

Website Design & Usability

Don't Make Me Think – Steve Krugg

Web Sites That Work – Jon Smith

Web Design In Easy Steps, 5th ed. – Sean McManus

Useit: www.useit.com/

Paid Search / PPC

Google Adwords That Work – Jon Smith

Advanced Google AdWords – Brad Geddes

www.google.com/adwords

https://adcenter.microsoft.com

http://advertisingcentral.yahoo.com

Viral Marketing

Viral loop: The power of pass it on – Adam Penenberg

The New Rules of Marketing and PR – David Meerman Scott

Flyer Printing & Design

www.onlineprinters.com

www.printingcenterusa.com/

www.flyerboy.com/

Company Formation Specialists

www.completeformations.co.uk

www.thecompanywarehouse.co.uk

www.companiesmadesimple.com

...cont'd

Venture Capital & Business Angels

UK **BVCA**: www.bvca.co.uk/home

USA **vFinance**: www.vfinance.com

www.advantagebusinessangels.com

www.bbaa.org.uk

Domain Names & Hosting

(USA) www.godaddy.com

(UK) www.123-reg.co.uk

Keyword & Phrase Research

www.wordtracker.com

https://adwords.google.com/select/KeywordToolExternal

(UK) www.hitwise.com

Search Directory

DMOZ www.dmoz.com

Open Source / Freemium Software

Essential 'Office' Software: www.openoffice.org

CRM Software: www.freecrm.com

Accounting Software: www.tassoftware.co.uk

Project Management: www.ganttproject.biz

...cont'd

Search Engine Optimization

Get into bed with Google – Jon Smith

Marketing in the age of Google – Vanessa Fox

50 Ways to Make Google Love Your Web Site – Steve Johnston

Related Books from the *In Easy Steps* series

Get to #1 on Google In Easy Steps – Ben Norman

Affiliate Networks

Affiliate Window www.affiliatewindow.com

TradeDoubler www.tradedoubler.com

Zanox www.zanox.com

Commission Junction www.cj.com

Online Marketplaces

Amazon.com www.amazon.com

Play.com www.play.com

eBay www.eBay.com

PriceMinister www.priceminister.co.uk

Freelancer Networks

Elance www.elance.com

People Per Hour www.peopleperhour.com

...cont'd

Blogging Tools

www.blogger.com

www.wordpress.com

Email Marketing Platforms

www.cheetahmail.com

www.dotmailer.co.uk

www.emaildem.com

Internet Marketing Agencies

Coast Digital: www.coastdigital.co.uk

Convert247: www.convert247.com

Eleven Marketing: www.11marketing.com

Internet E-Commerce Platforms

http://www.magento.com

http://www.oscommerce.com

http://www.zencart.com

http://www.virtuemart.net

http://www.dashcommerce.org

Online Payment Systems & Gateways

Paypal: www.paypal.com

Nochex: www.nochex.com

WorldPay: www.worldpay.com

SagePay: www.sagepay.com

RBSWorldpay: www.rbsworldpay.com

Internet Industry Research

www.mintel.com

www.forrester.co.uk

Social Media

www.delicious.com

http://digg.com

www.facebook.com

www.reddit.com

www.stumbleupon.com

http://technorati.com

www.twitter.com

www.linkedin.com

About The Author

Jon Smith is a digital strategist and writer. Part of the launch team for Amazon.co.uk and Kitbag.com Jon has been marketing websites and providing strategic advice to companies seeking to improve their online presence for over twelve years. He's launched, run and sold his own online businesses and has written extensively about website marketing and best-practice. Jon is the best-selling author of eleven books including *Get Into Bed With Google*, *Google Adwords That Work* and *Dominate Your Market With Twitter*.

Jon is co-founder and Director of Search at Convert247, a digital marketing agency operating in Barcelona, Spain.

Follow Jon on Twitter: @sanseng

More about Jon's books: www.jonsmith.net

Online Marketing and SEO consultancy: www.convert247.com

Other Books By Jon Smith

Smarter Business Start Ups (Infinite Ideas)

Web Sites That Work (Infinite Ideas)

Get Into Bed With Google: top ranking search optimization techniques (Infinite Ideas)

Be #1 on Google (McGraw-Hill)

Adwords That Work (Infinite Ideas)

Grow Your Business With Google Adwords (McGraw-Hill)

Dominate Your Market With Twitter (Infinite Ideas)

The Bloke's Guide To Pregnancy (Hay House)

The Bloke's Guide To Babies (Hay House)

The Bloke's Guide To Getting Hitched (Hay House)

The Bloke's Guide To Baby Gadgets (Hay House)

The Bloke's 100 Top Tips For Surviving Pregnancy (Hay House)

Toytopia (Wrecking Ball Press)

Index

N

O

P